INTO THE LAND OF
FREEDOM

INTO THE LAND OF
FREEDOM

AFRICAN AMERICANS IN RECONSTRUCTION

MEG GREENE

LERNER PUBLICATIONS COMPANY • MINNEAPOLIS

A Word about Language
The people who interviewed African Americans during the time of slavery and Reconstruction often recorded the speaker's dialect, or way of talking, as closely as possible. We have preserved dialect and original spellings, as well as the use of the now outdated term *negro*, in the quotations included in this book.

For Chip

Text copyright © 2004 by Meg Greene

Lerner Publications Company
A division of Lerner Publishing Group
241 First Avenue North
Minneapolis, MN 55401 U.S.A.

Website address: www.lernerbooks.com

Library of Congress Cataloging-in-Publication Data

Greene, Meg.
        Into the land of freedom: African Americans in Reconstruction / Meg Greene.
            p.   cm. — (People's history)
        Includes bibliographical references (p.) and index.
        ISBN: 0–8225–4690–6 (lib. bdg. : alk. paper)
            1. African Americans—History—1863–1877—Juvenile literature. 2. African Americans—Social conditions—19th century—Juvenile literature. 3. Freedmen—United States—History—19th century—Juvenile literature. 4. Reconstruction—Juvenile literature. [1. African Americans—History—1863–1877. 2. Reconstruction.] I. Title. II. Series: People's history.
        E185.2.G74 2004
        973'.0496073—dc22   2003018760

Manufactured in the United States of America
1 2 3 4 5 6 – JR – 09 08 07 06 05 04

Contents

THE DAY OF JUBILEE

We'll soon be free
We'll soon be free
We'll soon be free
When de Lord will call us home.
          —Slave spiritual,
        "Kingdom Comin'"

Young Robert Murray remembered exactly when life changed on the plantation where he lived and worked as a slave. It was the winter of 1860, and by early December, news had reached his master that Abraham Lincoln had been elected president of the United States. The mood on the plantation changed overnight. For Robert's master and other slave owners, Lincoln's election rang throughout the South like a warning bell of a coming crisis. Lincoln symbolized everything that white Southerners feared: a president who opposed slavery and a man who had the power to do something about it. Although the new president tried to reassure Southerners that he had no intention of abolishing, or ending, slavery, many slaveholders distrusted and hated him. And they worried that Lincoln's election would inspire their slaves to seek freedom.

Although only a boy, Robert began to notice his master and mistress eyeing him and the other slaves with suspicion. The slaves were being watched much more closely and had even less freedom than usual. More hurtful to Robert and the other slave children, perhaps, was the refusal of the master's family to let them visit the Big House (the master's home), as they once had. Unsure of why these sudden changes had come about and uncertain of their meaning, Robert turned to his mother for answers. "I know whut de trouble," she explained. "Dey s'pose we all wants ter be free."

"THE WORST DAYS THAT WAS EVER SEED BY THE WORLD"

Robert's mother was right. Black men, women, and children had been dreaming of a better, freer life since slave traders brought the first African slaves to North America in 1619. Some black people

The first ships carrying enslaved Africans landed at Jamestown, Virginia, in the early 1600s.

Under the control of drivers, enslaved African Americans return from the cotton fields carrying cotton bales. Slaves provided much of the labor necessary to keep the Southern economy—which was based on agriculture—operating.

later gained their freedom in the North, where slavery had been eventually outlawed. Others had been freed by their masters in the South. But thousands more were still enslaved in the 1800s. These slaves had little hope of being released from their bondage.

Some slave masters saw their slaves as human beings and even included them in their families. But in the eyes of the law—and to many slave owners—African American slaves were nothing more than property. As a result, many slave owners controlled almost every single moment of a slave's life, from the day the slave came into the world until the day the slave died. Slave owners also provided a slave's basic needs, such as shelter, food, and clothing. But in many cases, slaves were given barely enough to survive.

Most slaves labored for long hours every day except Sunday. They were told where they would work and even what kinds of jobs they would do. And white overseers or black drivers, who also were slaves, watched the slaves' every move as they toiled in the fields. Punishment came quickly and harshly if a slave failed to satisfy the overseer or the driver. Those slaves who worked inside the owner's home often were equally observed and punished by the master or mistress of the house. Mary Reynolds remembered her life as a field slave vividly:

> The conch shell blowed afore daylight and all hands better git out for roll call or Solomon bust the door down and git them out. It was work hard, git beatin's, and half-fed. . . . [There] never was as much [food] as we needed. . . . We prays for the end of trib'lation [suffering] and the end of beatin's and for shoes that fit our feet. . . . Some say [the slaves wished for] the time they's dead, 'cause they'd rather rot in the ground than have the beatin's.

Away from the long hours of work, slaves had little control over their personal lives. Their marriages were not considered legal, and they did not have the power to keep their families safe or together. Slave husbands and parents could not protect their wives and children from the master's whip. And slave owners could sell a slave's family members

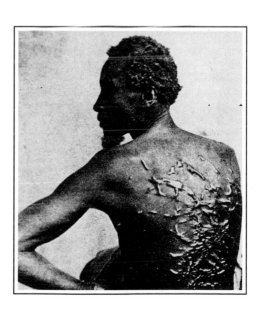

Many slave owners whipped their slaves as a form of discipline and control. The whippings often left horrible scarring.

Slave families were sold as property, and family members were often separated and sent to different plantations to work.

to other slaveholders whenever they wished. Many slaves were not even permitted to choose their own names or the names of their children.

For slaves who ran away or committed a crime against the owner, punishment was swift and brutal—sometimes even resulting in death. One of the greatest crimes a slave could commit was learning to read and write. Masters feared that knowledge would give their slaves the power to overthrow their owners and declare their freedom. As Mary Reynolds said, "Slavery was the worst days ever seed in the world. . . . I got the scars on my old body to show to this day."

"THE GREAT NATIONAL STRIFE"

On December 20, 1860, South Carolina seceded, or broke off from, the United States in protest of Lincoln's election and the possible abolition of slavery. Six other states—Mississippi, Florida, Alabama, Georgia,

Louisiana, and Texas—soon followed. These Southern states formed a new nation known as the Confederate States of America, or the Confederacy. The remaining Northern states were known as the Union.

On April 12, 1861, Confederate forces began the Civil War by bombarding federal (U.S.) troops stationed at Fort Sumter in South Carolina. When, on April 15, Lincoln called for 75,000 volunteers to put down what he called a rebellion, Virginia, Arkansas, North Carolina, and Tennessee left the Union as well. The country was soon to be torn apart by war.

AN UNCERTAIN TIME
For black men, women, and children, the outbreak of war brought feelings of both anxiety and hope. Generations of African Americans

The Confederate bombardment of Fort Sumter in South Carolina. The attack on the U.S. fort in 1861 marked the beginning of the Civil War.

had dreamed of the "day of jubilee," when they would at last stand free and equal to white Americans. At the beginning of the war, a free black man living in California thought he saw such a time drawing nearer:

> Everything among us indicates a change in our condition, and [we must] prepare to act in a different sphere from that in which we have heretofore acted. . . . Our relation to this government is changing daily. . . . Old things are passing away, and eventually old prejudices must follow. The revolution has begun, and time alone must decide where it is to end.

Yet, as one North Carolina plantation owner explained to his slave, the outcome of the struggle was far from certain for either North or

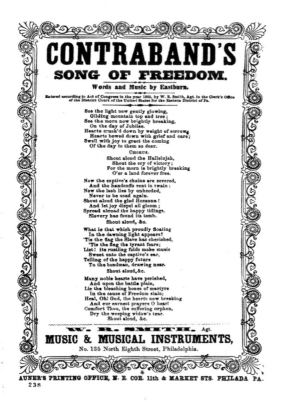

The much awaited "day of jubilee" is mentioned in the lyrics to this song about contrabands. Contrabands were slaves who escaped the South. Enslaved African Americans used song to tell their stories and lift their spirits.

In December 1862, Union troops were defeated at Fredericksburg, Virginia. This was one of many early battles signaling that the Confederacy might win and slavery continue.

South, black or white. "There is a war commenced between the North and the South. If the North whups [wins], you will be as free a man as I is. If the South whups, you will be a slave all your days."

"ARE, AND HENCEFORTH SHALL BE, FREE"

January 1, 1863, dawned cold in Washington, D.C., the capital of the United States of America. New Year's Day marked the beginning of the second winter of the Civil War. Many on both sides had thought the war would last no longer than three months. It even had been predicted that all the blood spilled in the Civil War would barely be enough to be absorbed by a lady's handkerchief or contained in a thimble.

By New Year's Day in 1863, few people in Washington were in the mood for merrymaking. A few weeks earlier, the South had inflicted a humiliating defeat on Union forces at Fredericksburg, Virginia. The war was going badly, and there were no signs of it ending soon. New Year's Eve had found the streets of Washington virtually deserted.

President Lincoln marked the turn of the year with a combination of work and recreation. He welcomed guests to the traditional New Year's

Day reception at the White House. But by midafternoon, Lincoln left the festivities and returned to his office. There, an important document, the Emancipation Proclamation, awaited his signature.

The document, an early draft of which Lincoln had issued in September 1862, was short—only five pages and written out on narrow sheets of paper in black ink. Like other official government papers, it would be bound up in red and blue ribbon when the president had finished signing it. Then it would be fastened shut with the wax seal of the United States. Yet the ordinary appearance of the document disguised its importance, for in it Lincoln had granted freedom to approximately three million slaves.

In the Emancipation Proclamation, Lincoln declared "that all persons held as slaves" within those states that had seceded from the Union and

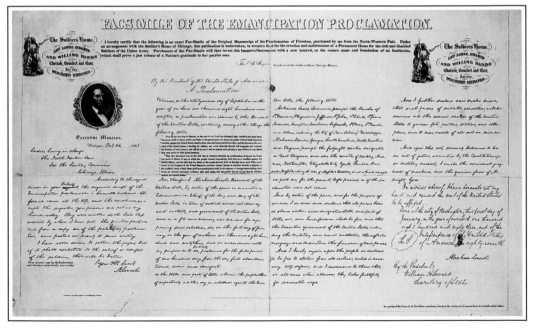

A copy of the Emancipation Proclamation in President Lincoln's handwriting. The presidential proclamation declared that the slaves were to be free, but the South fought to keep them in bondage.

continued in a state of rebellion "are, and henceforward shall be, free." It was a powerful statement, and the promise it held echoed throughout the nation long after the war was over.

Lincoln had not at first made the abolition of slavery an aim of the war. Restoring the Union, with or without slavery, had been his chief goal. But eventually he realized that putting an end to slavery would destroy the Southern economy. The loss of the labor that African American slaves provided for Southern plantations and many households would be devastating to the South. Lincoln issued the Emancipation Proclamation only when he was convinced that destroying slavery meant destroying the Confederacy.

Yet the Emancipation Proclamation itself freed no one. The slaves to whom Lincoln granted freedom were those who lived in the Confederate States of America. Lincoln had no legal authority or control over the Confederacy. A Union victory was required for emancipation—the freeing of all slaves—to be complete.

THE GRAPEVINE TELEGRAPH

Although not actually freeing a single slave, the Emancipation Proclamation altered the nature and meaning of the Civil War. Karl Marx, a German political and economic scholar, reported on the war from the European perspective. As an overseas correspondent for Greeley's *New York Tribune,* Marx understood the revolutionary significance of Lincoln's proclamation. In an essay entitled "On Events in North America," originally published in *Die Presse* (an Austrian newspaper) on October 12, 1862, Marx declared that "the Emancipation Proclamation [is] the most significant document in American history since the founding of the Union and one which tears up the old American Constitution."

News of the proclamation spread quickly throughout the South. On many plantations, slaves relayed the news to one another by word of mouth. The message was carried from plantation to plantation through the so-called Grapevine Telegraph, a network of messengers that existed among slaves. In some cases, slaves organized groups such as the Lincoln's Loyal League in Mississippi to spread the news from plantation to plantation.

When news of the Emancipation Proclamation reached the plantations, some slaves quit working immediately and took the risk of running away to freedom. Others, deciding to stay for the time being, showed less willingness to carry out their usual tasks. In some cases, they treated their owners with barely hidden anger and resentment.

The way slaves expressed their religious faith began to change too. Faith had long helped slaves get through rough times. Yet they were usually forbidden to organize their own prayer meetings and were forced to gather in secret in the middle of the night. These prayer meetings became bolder, as black activist Booker T. Washington remembered. "[They] had more ring, and lasted later into the night." The slaves sang spirituals, songs that spoke of freedom and deliverance to heaven, with more gusto and intensity than ever before. As Washington wrote, they were no longer "afraid to let it be known that the 'freedom' in their songs meant freedom of the body in this world." They were dreaming of freedom not in heaven but on earth.

An escaped family of slaves races toward the freedom of a Union state. Though escaped slaves sometimes reached freedom in the North, slaveholders had the legal right to reclaim their "property."

Freed and escaped slaves sought refuge with the Union army. Many of them joined the army to fight for a free, unified country.

"OUR BONDAGE IS OVER"

After January 1, 1863, every Union victory moved enslaved black people one step closer to freedom. Because Lincoln was dedicated both to ending slavery and to preserving the Union, many slaves saw him as their liberator. Most important, perhaps, from the slaves' point of view, Lincoln's proclamation announced that black people could play an active role in bringing about their own emancipation. Runaway slaves would be granted automatic freedom by enlisting in the Union army or navy and taking part in conquering the South. One black Union soldier who entered the Confederacy's capital, Richmond, Virginia, near the end of the war, announced to his enslaved brothers and sisters: "We have come to set you free!"

As the Union soldiers marched through the South, they often met enslaved African American men, women, and children fleeing to freedom and safety behind the Union lines. During the two years following the proclamation, approximately 200,000 African Americans from both the North and the South fought on the side of the Union.

Still, others aided the North's cause by acting as spies. Early in 1864, one Confederate officer complained that the slave spy network seemed to be everywhere and unstoppable. Time and again, the black spies searched out the secret war plans of the Confederacy and shared them with the Union army.

For some former slaves, aiding the Union forces turned into a family affair. Men served in the military as soldiers or spies, while women did the cooking and laundry for both black and white troops. Soon small shantytowns (poor communities) housing former slaves and their families appeared on the edges of U.S. military camps.

The opportunity to help gain their own freedom was exhilarating for many slaves. George W. Hatton, a sergeant in the U.S. Colored Troops, fought in the last battles of the war during 1864 and 1865. On one occasion, he wrote, "I look around me and see hundreds of colored men armed and ready to defend the Government at any moment; and such are my feelings that I can only say, the fetters [chains] have fallen—our bondage is over."

In May 1864, Hatton's regiment made camp not far from Jamestown, Virginia. Here, as many of the soldiers noted, "the first sons of Africa," had set foot on American soil more than two centuries before. It was in Jamestown, too, that many of the black troops had formerly worked as slaves.

Hatton recalled one incident in which the black soldiers took small revenge on one of their masters. While searching for food, the soldiers captured "a Mr. Clayton, a noted reb [Southern rebel] in this part of the country," who had earlier viciously whipped several of his female slaves. Seeking the protection of federal troops, the women had escaped to Hatton's regiment the day before. One soldier named William Harris was one of Clayton's former slaves. Tying Clayton to a tree and stripping him of his clothes, Harris gave Clayton twenty strokes of the lash. He then handed the whip to each of the women, who also each gave Clayton several strokes. The whippings were, Hatton later wrote, a powerful reminder to Clayton.

[His former slaves] were no longer his, but safely [under Lincoln's protection] and under the protection of the Star-Spangled Banner, and guarded by their own patriotic, though once down-trodden race. . . . Oh, that I had the tongue to express my feelings, while standing upon the banks of the James River, on the soil of Virginia, the mother state of slavery, as a witness of such a sudden reverse. The day is clear, the fields of grain are beautiful, and the birds are singing sweet melodious songs, while poor Mr. C. is crying to his servants for mercy.

KINGDOM COMIN'

As thousands of slaves flocked to join the Union army, others, still at work on plantations throughout the South, closely followed the news of the war. Many either openly or secretly cheered the triumphs of Union forces.

On some plantations, the elation and excitement of the slaves was evident. On others, though, the slaves went about their work as if nothing special had taken place. Their apparent indifference puzzled slave owners. In 1865 federal troops under the command of General William Tecumseh Sherman marched into South Carolina. One wealthy planter wrote that his slaves were "as silent as they had been in April, 1861, when they heard from a distance the opening guns of war. . . . Did those Negroes know that their freedom was so near? I cannot say, but, if they did, they said nothing, only patiently waited to see what would come." Another planter wrote that his slaves were as "orderly and respectful" as could be expected "under the circumstances." In her diary, Mary Boykin Chesnut wondered whether the slaves were "solidly stupid, or wiser than we are, silent and strong, biding their time?"

In fact, many slaves were waiting for Union soldiers, their "liberators," to show themselves. At once excited and terrified, the slaves listened to the sound of the North's cannons, echoing in their ears and coming closer each day. To young Sam Mitchell of South Carolina,

Union and Confederate artillery fire erupts around a plantation home.
For many slaves, the sound of artillery signaled that freedom was near.

the cannon fire, as his mother told him, "ain't no t'under, dat Yankee [Northerner] come to gib you Freedom." Annie Osborne, a young slave living in Louisiana, thought that the cannons meant "We's gwine be all freed from old Massa Tom's beatings." When Sarah Debro, a slave in North Carolina, asked what the loud booming noises were, the answers she received summed up the feelings of both slaves and masters. First, her white mistress, crying, explained that the "thunder" Sarah heard was, in fact, artillery fire killing Confederate soldiers. Then Sarah's Aunt Charity took her aside and revealed the real reason her mistress was crying. "She ain't cryin kaze de Yankees killin'de mens, she's doin all dat cryin' kaze she skeered we's goin' to be [set] free."

The dramatic events the slaves were hearing and witnessing seemed to be sent to them from the Lord above. Seldom had their prayers been answered so directly and concretely as when Northern soldiers at last marched onto their plantations. The soldiers entered the "big house" and ordered the master and mistress to set all the black men, women, and children free. An elderly slave woman from Savannah, Georgia, declared sentiments that matched the feelings of countless other freed slaves.

I'd always thought about this, and wanted this day to come, and prayed for it and knew God meant it should be here sometime, but I didn't believe I should ever see it, and it is so great and good a thing, I cannot believe it has come now; and I don't believe I shall ever realize it, but I know it has though, and I bless the Lord for it.

At the end of the war, General Sherman marched his Union forces from Atlanta toward the sea and then turned northward into the Carolinas. He was followed by thousands of freed men, women, and children who abandoned their plantations to join the Union soldiers on their triumphant journey through the conquered South. Sherman later wrote that the slaves flocked to him, "old and young, they pray[ed] and shout[ed] and mix[ed] up my name with Moses and Simon [biblical heroes] . . . [and] 'Abram Linkom,' the Great Messiah of 'Dis Jubilee.'"

Former slaves were among the victorious Union troops who marched with General Sherman into Charleston, South Carolina, in 1865.

After the Civil War ended, some former slaves remained on the plantations where they had once been enslaved.

For all the black people who joyously celebrated their freedom, there were those who could not quite comprehend what was happening. William Hutson, a Georgia slave, recalled that his master told him and others that they were free. Then his master asked them to stay until they had finished harvesting his crops. Hutson and the others discussed the master's proposal. Hutson recalled that "they wasn't no celebration 'round the place. . . . Nobody leave the place though. Not 'till the fall when the work is through." A slave in Tennessee remembered how the plantation overseer had come into the fields to tell them that they were all free. Several slaves asked, "Free, how?" It was a question that many African Americans sought to answer in the coming years.

RECONSTRUCTING A NATION

With a Northern victory in sight, President Lincoln tried to figure out how best to bring the Confederate states back into the Union after the war. Reuniting the North and the South had always been his goal.

Yet Lincoln also realized that there was more involved in this task than merely readmitting the Southern states. The South needed to be "reconstructed," or built again. Since most of the war had been fought in the South, the region was devastated. Many Southern cities, such as the capital at Richmond, Virginia, were in ruins. The rural areas were often nothing more than scorched earth. One visitor to Columbia, South Carolina, another city particularly hard hit by Union troops, described the sight as "a wilderness of crumbling walls, naked chimneys, and trees killed by flames." Lincoln faced a difficult task and certainly one of his greatest challenges.

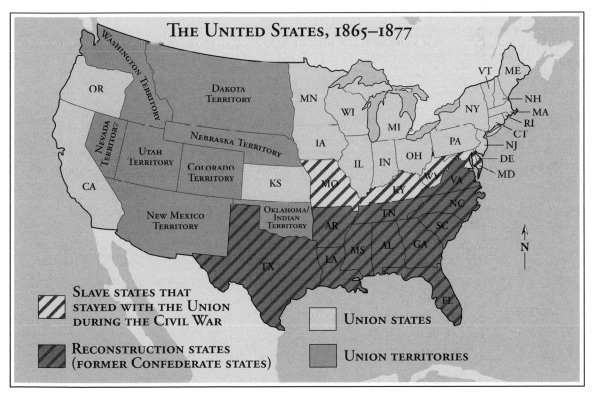

The divided United States at the end of the Civil War and during Reconstruction. Former Confederate states were slowly readmitted to the Union during Reconstruction. Nebraska became a state in 1867.

Lincoln believed that it was the task of the president and not Congress to decide the terms and conditions under which the rebel Southern states would be allowed back into the Union. According to Lincoln's plan of Reconstruction, any former Confederate state could rejoin the Union under one condition. Ten percent of its eligible voters had to swear their loyalty to the federal government and the U.S. Constitution.

But many Republican members of Congress believed that white Southerners, especially the wealthiest slaveholders, should be punished for their rebellion. These congressmen believed that many people in the South, even after they swore allegiance to the United States, would not be loyal citizens. They also feared that many white Southerners would not honor the rights of freed slaves. Instead of adopting Lincoln's generous plan, Congress tried to enact its own tougher version of Reconstruction. Lincoln, however, vetoed Congress's plan.

During this time, the federal government also enacted two important pieces of legislation that leaders hoped would strengthen the promise Lincoln had made in the Emancipation Proclamation. In January 1865, Congress passed the Thirteenth Amendment, which abolished slavery throughout the United States and recognized the freedom of African Americans. (The amendment became part of the Constitution in December 1865.) Having been residents of the United States for more than two hundred years, African Americans at last took their first steps toward full citizenship.

On March 3, 1865, another important piece of legislation was passed, creating the Bureau of Refugees, Freedmen, and Abandoned Lands. This agency became known as the Freedman's Bureau, and its job was to help former slaves make the transition to freedom. The government intended the bureau to "last during the present War of the Rebellion [the Civil War], and for one year thereafter." The bureau hired white civilians and soldiers. It faced a daunting task: to help former slaves and other poor people throughout the South. The bureau's goal was to give these citizens the tools to support themselves and the power to run their own lives.

*U.S. leaders celebrate the passing of the Thirteenth Amendment, **left**. Following its passage, Frederick Douglass, **right**, warned that much more would have to be done to make former slaves truly free. Douglass, a former slave, spoke out for African American rights.*

In addition to providing food and medical care, the bureau also provided education for the newly freed slaves. Some members of Congress, such as the staunch abolitionist Thaddeus Stevens, also hoped that the bureau would help break up former slave plantations and divide the land among African Americans. The North had taken these lands from Confederates throughout the South during the Civil War. Stevens hoped that forty-acre plots would automatically be given to each adult freedman, or ex-slave, to farm.

"THE DAY OF JUBILEE"

Then at last the war was over. On April 9, 1865, General Robert E. Lee, commander of the Army of Northern Virginia, surrendered to Union general Ulysses S. Grant at the home of Wilmer McLean in Appomattox Court House, Virginia. For the majority of African Americans, the end of the war marked the beginning of a new life, with many difficult challenges ahead. "Verily," said the former slave and noted abolitionist Frederick Douglass, "the work does not end with abolition of slavery, but only begins."

HOW FREE IS FREE?

*If I cannot do like a white man I
am not free.*
   —former slave Henry Adams to
                     his master, 1865

"Freedom," a black minister once said, "burned in the black heart long before freedom was born." For many African Americans, the end of the Civil War was not only an end to their lives as an enslaved people, it was also the start of a new life full of promise and peril. No longer did they need to fear their masters' power. The early morning bells that summoned them to their work and often measured out the hours of their day lay silent. They were free to move about, to visit, to worship, and to work as they chose. Yet, as one former slave from Virginia recalled, the feelings of freedom were more complex than simple exhilaration:

> They [African Americans] were like a bird let out of a cage.
> You know how a bird that has been long in the cage will
> act when the door is opened; he makes a curious fluttering

for a little while. It was just so with colored people. They didn't know at first what to do with themselves. But they got sobered pretty soon.

Beneath the joyous celebrations were questions and doubts. What did it mean to be free? How did one live as a freedman? Could the former slaves survive without their masters' help? Would their former owners and other white Southerners recognize and respect black rights? Would they be safe? These and other concerns lessened the joy of the former slaves as they set out to create new lives for themselves among a hostile white community.

"SLAVERY IS DEAD"

At the end of the war, the editor of a Georgia newspaper expressed the feelings of many white Southerners when he declared:

> The different races of man, like different coins at a mint, were stamped at their true value by the Almighty [God] in the beginning. No contact with each other—no amount of legislation or education—can convert the negro into a white man.... The negro cannot claim equality with the white race.

A recently freed family sets out to create a new life, faced with an uncertain future.

The editor of a Cincinnati newspaper put the matter even more bluntly when he wrote, "Slavery is dead, the negro is not, there is the misfortune. For the sake of all parties, would that he were."

Many white Southerners did not believe that their former slaves were able to take on the responsibilities of freedom. South Carolinian Julius J. Fleming stated that newly freed African Americans "do not understand the liberty that has been conferred upon [given to] them." The director of the Freedmen's Bureau, former Union general Oliver O. Howard, warned his black audience in 1865 that freedom was "apt [likely] to be misunderstood." As Howard explained to his listeners, they were not to expect the same kind of treatment that white citizens enjoyed.

But many freedmen, such as former slave and minister Henry Turner, had a very clear idea of what freedom meant. It was not just being free from the shackles of slavery. It was also the opportunity to

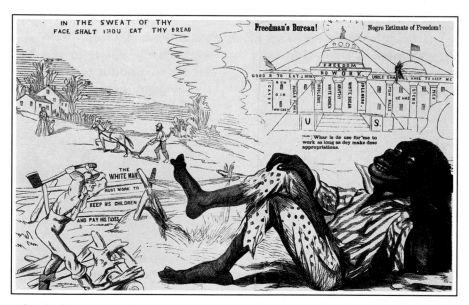

This highly racist political cartoon shows white men hard at work while a black man relaxes under the protection of the government and the Freedman's Bureau. The cartoon reflects a Reconstruction belief that the U.S. government gave freedmen more power than whites and allowed them to be lazy.

Confederate sympathizer and assassin John Wilkes Booth takes aim at an unsuspecting Lincoln in the presidential box of Ford's Theatre.

enjoy their "rights in common with other men." Many African Americans hoped President Lincoln and other Northern leaders would help protect those important rights.

A FATEFUL EVENING

On Good Friday, April 14, 1865, President Lincoln was looking forward to a relaxing evening away from the exciting but exhausting days that had just passed. The war had ended six days earlier. Since then, Lincoln's life had been a whirlwind of activity. His only thoughts, though, were to accompany his wife to a performance of the comedy *Our American Cousin* at Ford's Theatre in Washington, D.C. But Lincoln's evening ended tragically. At 10:15 P.M., John Wilkes Booth, a twenty-six-year-old actor sympathetic to the Confederacy, sneaked up behind Lincoln and shot him in the back of the head. Booth then jumped from the presidential box to the stage, breaking his leg in the fall. He shouted "Sic semper tyrannis! [Thus always to tyrants!] The South is avenged!" He hobbled away before the stunned actors could capture him. Lincoln died at 7:22 the following morning, without regaining consciousness.

Throughout the nation, people were shocked and horrified when they learned of Lincoln's murder. For the former slaves, Lincoln's death was especially tragic. Many had seen him as the man responsible for their freedom. Throughout the South, thousands of former slaves mourned. Many wore black on their clothing, such as one young woman who sewed strips of black cloth around the bottom of her dress. One former slave turned his coat inside out to show the black lining as a symbol of his grief. African Americans in Mitchellville, South Carolina, wore armbands of black cloth on their left arms for the rest of April. Those who had no black cloth or who could not afford to buy any are said to have taken flour sacks and dipped them in chimney soot to make them black. Most every African American community mourned Lincoln in some way.

Many white Southerners also wondered what lay ahead for them. They knew that Lincoln was more forgiving of their actions than some members of Congress. Jefferson Davis, the former president of the Confederacy, summarized their fears. He said that "next to the destruction of the Confederacy, the death of Abraham Lincoln was the darkest day the South has ever known."

"OUR FREEDOM"

As African Americans mourned the loss of the president, they continued to make sense of what it meant to "live free." For some, such as Houston Holloway, freedom meant welcoming his freeborn son into the world. Freedman Charlie Barbour thought that the promise of a free life meant "dat I won't wake up some mornin'ter fin' dat my mammy or some ob de rest of my family am done sold." For others freedom was the simple act of walking away from the plantation or meeting in the open to conduct religious services. Often the former slaves gathered to talk about "our freedom" and what new opportunities, problems, prospects, and responsibilities it offered.

To celebrate their new lives, some freedmen and freedwomen wished to be rid of the names given to them by their owners. Freedpersons usually chose a new first and last name. Often their inspiration came from the names of famous Americans. A schoolteacher in Savannah, Georgia, for example, reported that among her black pupils were an Alexander Hamilton, a Franklin Pierce, and a Thomas Jefferson. Other African Americans changed their names to show the promise of their new status, giving rise to names such as Deliverance Berlin, Hope Mitchell, and Chance Great. Some were more skeptical or, at least, were taking no chances. They changed their names just in case white Southerners reestablished slavery. They reasoned that they would be much harder to track down if they were going by a different name.

Abolitionist and former slave Sojourner Truth was a role model for many freedpersons who wanted to change their names. Born into slavery as Isabella Baumfree, she changed her name after escaping slavery and having a spiritual revelation, telling her to preach the Gospel and the message of freedom. Her new name, like that of many freedpersons, reflected her sense of who she was: a traveler who spread truth.

Some freed African Americans kept their slave names, not from feelings of sentimentality toward their former masters, but as a way of acknowledging their black families. As one ex-slave explained, he kept his master's last name because it was also the name his mother and father had. Much to the agitation of white Southerners, many emancipated black people also made it known that they wished to be addressed more formally as "mister" or "missus," rather than by their first names, as had been the custom under slavery. No matter whether the freedmen held onto their former names or adopted new ones, they believed they should have the choice to do whatever they wished.

IN THE EYES OF THE LAW

On many plantations, slave couples had been unofficially married in ceremonies conducted by their masters. But these unions were not recognized by the law. Many freedmen and freedwomen quickly acted to make their marriages legal. With the encouragement of black ministers

Following the Civil War, many freedpersons were legally married, which had been impossible under slavery.

Legal marriages gave freedpersons the legal right to determine the future of their children and families.

and white missionaries (people sent to a place to do religious work and to convert others to their faith), black couples throughout the South retook their marriage vows. They walked away with marriage licenses and proof that they were legally married.

For many ex-slaves, however, retaking marriage vows was not only an effort to have their unions recognized by law. It was also an important step in making sure that the law recognized their rights as parents to take charge of their children's lives. Mass wedding ceremonies, which in some cases involved as many as seventy couples, became common throughout the South during Reconstruction. A witness described these ceremonies and their symbolic importance:

> One evening four couples came to the schoolhouse to meet "the parson" who was to perform their marriage ceremony for them. They came straight from the field, in their working clothes; the women, as was their custom, walking behind the men. . . . When they left the schoolhouse the women all took their places by the side of the men, showing that they [the couple] felt they were equal [to white couples] in the eyes of the law.

Yet emancipation also complicated family relations, as former slaves started their new life in freedom. Many men and women had been married as slaves only to be separated when the master sold one or both of them to different owners. They sometimes married again on their new plantations and raised new families. In such cases, the couples faced a tangled web of family connections after emancipation. The former slaves had to decide which marriage and family obligations they would honor. If such a choice proved impossible, African Americans sometimes found unique solutions to the problem. In South Carolina, for example, a woman alternated between two spouses who lived in separate locations. The laws of many Southern states, however, required ex-slaves to choose one spouse.

Sometimes officials of the Freedmen's Bureau made the choice for them, especially when children were involved. One bureau official in North Carolina reported: "Whenever a negro appears before me with two or three wives who have equal claim upon him, I marry him to the woman who has the greatest number of helpless children."

JOYFUL REUNIONS

Among the most powerful scenes to take place across the Reconstruction South were the reunions of slave families. For many African Americans, life under slavery had not simply meant hard work, harsh treatment, and injustice. Slavery had also disrupted family life. Many families had been broken apart when family members were sold, and few entertained realistic hopes of ever seeing their loved ones again. Yet, despite the long odds against success, many former slaves set out in search of the families they had lost.

Former slaves who could read and write were asked to write letters in the hope of finding long-lost relatives. The letters were often sent to the plantations where the slave had been sold or to other former slaves who might have information about a missing loved one. Missionaries and teachers from the North also wrote letters for freed slaves to help them track down the people whom slavery had stolen from them.

Sometimes former slaves found family members in one of the many refugee camps that the Freedmen's Bureau set up throughout the South. These camps housed people who had left their plantations and had nowhere else to live. A chance meeting at a camp reunited Ben and Betty Dodson, a husband and wife who had been separated for almost twenty years. One young Tennessee woman had been a child when her mother was sold to another master. She found her mother years later in a refugee camp, recognizing her only because of the scar she remembered on her mother's face. In a Virginia refugee camp,

Some couples, like the one above and the one mentioned in an old Ohio newspaper at right, were reunited after years of separation under slavery. For many freedpersons, however, happy reunions never came.

Reunited After Forty Years.

Dayton, O.—Randall Bogie, now aged 74, of Springfield, and Mrs. Celia Harnady, aged 59, were married years ago in Madison county, Ky., when slaves. Some time before the war Mrs. Bogie with an infant in her arms, was sold and taken far south. Bogie, broken-hearted over the separation joined the Union army, and at the close of the war was in Texas. Ten years later Bogie returned to Kentucky only to find that his wife had moved over into Ohio and married one Harnady. Bogie shortly afterward married another wife who died last June. Mr. Harnady died four years ago, and in the course of time both of the lovers drifted north, Harnady locating in this city and Mr. Bogie going to Springfield. Left alone in the world, the old persons began to think fondly again of each other, with the result that they soon arranged a meeting, and the old man began to court his former wife again with all the ardor that he showed in his youth. This courtship terminated in another marriage, their second one, which was performed recently by Rev. Grant, of this city.

a mother discovered her eighteen-year-old daughter, taken from her when the girl was still an infant. The woman's joy at finding her daughter was dulled by her anger at seeing her daughter's face disfigured from the beatings she had received at the hands of her master.

Other searches led nowhere or revealed the sad fate a loved one had suffered. An agent for the Freedmen's Bureau remarked that "every mother's son . . . seemed to be in search of his mother, every mother in search of her children. In their eyes the work of emancipation was incomplete." For many it would always remain so. In North Carolina, a Northern journalist came upon an elderly black man walking by the side of the road. The man told the reporter that he had already walked six hundred miles in search of his wife and children, who had been sold four years earlier. He had not yet found them. Relying on the smallest bit of information, many African Americans continued to search in vain for their loved ones. For most no happy reunion took place.

A "WORKING CLASS OF PEOPLE"

For black men and women who had kept or reestablished their families, the abolition of slavery created a new challenge. It was up to them to provide for their loved ones. White Southerners liked to predict that free African Americans either could not or would not work without supervision and the threat of punishment. For freedmen and freedwomen, this idea was not only false but insulting. As one Alabama freedman angrily asked, "Whence comes the assertion [from where comes the claim] that the [freedman] won't work? It comes from this fact: . . . the freedman refuses to be driven out into the field two hours before day, and work until 9 or 10 o'clock in the night." African Americans were happy to work, as long as they would be treated fairly and receive a just wage for their labor.

Many white people accused African Americans of being nothing but lazy. One freedman responded that if anybody could be described as lazy, it was their former masters. After all, he said, it was the slave

Freedpersons welcomed the rights to work for themselves, to choose what work they did, and to decide what wage was fair for their labor.

owners who had "lived in idleness all their lives on stolen labor." One Virginia freedman simply stated that "he who makes [the claim that black people are lazy] asserts [says] an untruth. We have been working all our lives, not only supporting ourselves, but we have supported our masters, many of them in idleness." Another freedman agreed that "we used to support ourselves and our master too when we were slaves and I reckon we can take care of ourselves now."

In order to support their families, former slaves either had to acquire land or find work. As much as possible, freedmen and freedwomen aimed to control their working conditions. After a lifetime of sweating to make other men rich, African Americans were eager to work for themselves. "They will almost starve and go naked before they will work for a white man," declared one Georgia planter.

During the early days of Reconstruction, many former slaves refused to work in situations where they would be directed by a white overseer. Such arrangements were too similar to slavery. A Georgia landowner learned this lesson the hard way when he hired a white overseer in 1865 and then watched in disbelief as the black workers left his fields untended.

FORMING FREE FAMILIES

African Americans also took control of their private lives. Under slavery, many women had labored in the fields alongside men. After emancipation, men and women split duties along the more traditional lines that white men and women followed. For men that meant heavier work, such as plowing, splitting rails, and tending the fields. The duties of black women centered more in the home. There they kept busy cooking, cleaning, and raising children.

In many families of former slaves, women took care of the home and children, and men did heavy work.

Many freedmen did not permit their wives to work outside the home. This change had an unexpected result: many white Southerners discovered that an important group of workers, black women, had been lost to them. One newspaper editor complained that black women would no longer "pick cotton, which is a woman's work. . . . They will merely take care of their own households and do but little or no work outdoors." When planters in one area of Louisiana tried to force black women into the fields to work, freedmen stepped in telling the planters, "whenever [the black men] wanted their wives to work they would tell them themselves; and if [they] could not rule [their] own domestic affairs on that place [they] would leave it."

Black women also were reluctant to take on work as domestic servants in white people's homes, for fear of being treated poorly. Those who did made it clear that they would return to their own homes at the end of the workday and would not be living in their employer's house. The refusal of the freedwomen to work often met with criticism and hostility from white Southerners. Black housewives were seen as lazy and foolish for "acting the *lady*."

Black men and women also for the first time took more control over the parenting of their children. Under slavery, the master decided when the children would work and what they would do. Many freed parents refused to allow their children to work at all, insisting instead that they attend one of the schools that the Freedmen's Bureau promised to set up. White employers resented not being able to force black children into the fields to work. As one Georgia newspaper reported, "The freedmen have almost universally withdrawn their women and children from the fields, putting the first at housework and the latter at school."

The freedom to make decisions about their families was an important step in strengthening and stabilizing the African American family, but it was only the beginning. It would take the federal government to protect the rights and freedoms that African Americans were due as true citizens of the United States.

"GIVE US THIS, AND WE WILL PROTECT OURSELVES"

*The future looks dark, and we pre-
dict, that we are entering upon the
greatest political contest that has
ever agitated the people of the
country—a contest, in which, we
of the South must be for the most
part spectators; not indifferent
spectators for it is about us that the
political battle is fought.*
—unidentified African American
newspaper article, 1866

After the Civil War, the writer and abolitionist Frederick Douglass, who had escaped from slavery, offered the American people a
piece of advice. Leave black people alone, Douglass said. In one of
his most inspired speeches, he said:

> If you see [a black person] plowing in the open field, leveling
> the forest, at work with a spade, a rake, a hoe, a pick-axe, or
> a bill—let him alone; he has a right to work. If you see him
> on his way to school, with spelling book, geography and
> arithmetic in his hands—let him alone. . . . If he has a ballot
> in his hand, and is on his way to the ballot-box to deposit
> his vote for the man whom he thinks will most justly and
> wisely administer the Government which has the power of
> life and death over him, as well as others—let him *alone*.

But Douglass, like other supporters of Reconstruction, did not wish the federal government to leave African Americans alone. Douglass believed that only the government could ensure the rights that had been promised to them. He believed the government should not abandon African Americans but had to make sure that they all had the right to work, to learn, and to vote.

A NEW PRESIDENT, AN OLD PLAN

Vice President Andrew Johnson, a former tailor, shopkeeper, and slave owner from Tennessee, believed strongly in bringing together the divided Union. He had become president after Lincoln's assassination, and he meant to continue Lincoln's generous policies of Reconstruction. Like Lincoln, he focused more on helping restore the bond between the North and the South than on protecting the rights of newly freed African Americans.

In this political cartoon, President Andrew Johnson seems to be helping a freedperson. In contrast, evidence of his hands-off approach to civil rights appears throughout the cartoon. Johnson, a former slave owner, was caught between angry Southerners and strong supporters of Reconstruction. He often seemed neither to support nor to oppose freedpersons and civil rights.

Johnson put his Reconstruction program into effect during the summer of 1865, while Congress was not in session. But some members of Congress strongly believed that planning Reconstruction was, or ought to be, a congressional privilege.

The following year, Congress took action and passed the Civil Rights Act of 1866. This law based citizenship on country of birth, rather than race, and provided for equal protection under the law for all citizens. That same year, Congress drafted the Fourteenth Amendment to the Constitution. The Amendment guarantees the rights of

A draft of the Fourteenth Amendment to the U.S. Constitution, establishing citizenship and equal protection under the law to all Americans regardless of race. This draft was penned in 1866.

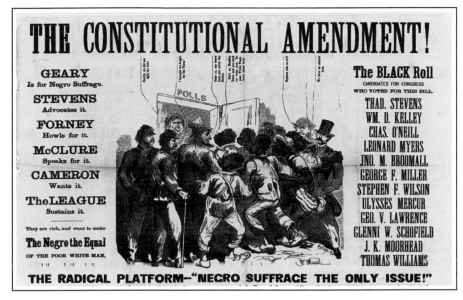

Freedmen race into a Southern voting station under the protection of U.S. troops in this racist political cartoon. The cartoon warns white voters not to back candidates who support greater rights for freedmen, especially suffrage, or the right to vote.

citizenship and equal protection under the law to all Americans, regardless of race. It was eventually adopted in 1868.

Some Republicans in Congress, such as Representative Thaddeus Stevens of Pennsylvania and Senators Charles Sumner of Massachusetts and Benjamin Wade of Ohio, went a step further. Called Radical, or extreme, Republicans by pro-South legislators, these men pushed for and won passage of a Reconstruction bill that divided the South into five military districts and appointed governors to each district. The bill also ordered federal troops to be stationed in the South to assist the governors when needed.

District governors would have the power to make sure that black voters and white voters alike could elect men to represent them at state conventions. The large meetings would be organized to create new state constitutions (official documents that list states' basic laws).

Freedmen vote for the first time in 1867. Although the right of freedmen to vote was not yet granted by the U.S. Constitution, the Reconstruction Act of 1867 required former Confederate states to rewrite their constitutions to allow freedmen to vote.

The new constitutions had to abolish slavery and ensure the rights of African Americans. A majority of black voters and white voters had to approve the new state constitutions, and Congress also had to ratify (approve) them. Finally, before former Confederate states could rejoin the Union, state legislatures (law-making groups) had to adopt the Fourteenth Amendment.

Johnson vetoed the Radical Republicans' Reconstruction bill, but Congress overrode the president's veto. The Reconstruction Act passed on March 2, 1867. For the time being, the U.S. government would work to preserve the rights of African Americans.

"THE GREAT SENSATION OF THE DAY"

In state legislatures across the South, elected men gathered to change the old state constitutions. A decade earlier, such an event would have been unthinkable. Southern states would have been unwilling to rewrite their constitutions and give African Americans the rights of citizens.

These constitutional conventions were, as one newspaper reporter noted, "the great sensation of the day" and a sign of "great and dreaded innovations."

What made these events all the more remarkable was that each of the Southern constitutional conventions included some black members. In South Carolina, the birthplace of secession, there were more black delegates than white. In Louisiana an equal number of black men and white men took part. Some of the convention members were former slaves, while others had been free all their lives. Still other black representatives who had been born in the North had come to the South only after the war. All were considered moderate in their political views. A reporter for the *Charleston Daily News* of South Carolina offered this description of the black delegates at the South Carolina convention:

> Considering the influences under which they were called together, and their [limited knowledge of the] law, they have displayed for the most part, remarkable moderation and dignity. . . . They have assembled neither to pull wires like some, nor to make money like others, but to [stand up] for the welfare of the race to which they belong.

John W. Menard became the first African American voted into the U.S. Congress. The people of Louisiana elected him to the U.S. House of Representatives in 1868. But the House did not accept him as a representative.

The state constitutions drawn up during 1867 and 1868 brought about dramatic and sweeping changes in Southern political life. Among other important innovations, the new constitutions stated that men no longer had to own property in order to vote or hold political office. This important change opened the way for the participation of black men in political affairs.

With no previous experience, African Americans became actively involved in Reconstruction. They served as delegates to the constitutional conventions and were elected to a variety of state and federal political offices. Twenty black men took seats in the U.S. House of Representatives between 1869 and 1901. Two men, Blanche K. Bruce of Virginia and Hiram Revels of Mississippi, won election to the U.S. Senate.

Between black voters and white Republican voters, the new Reconstruction governments received widespread and enthusiastic support. Yet despite the complaint of white Southerners against "Negro rule" in the South, African Americans never controlled these governments. The Reconstruction governments supported civil rights because they had no choice. Without African Americans, the pro-Reconstruction Republicans could not hold onto power.

Mississippi voters elected Hiram Revels, **left,** *to the U.S. Senate in 1870, and Virginians sent Blanche K. Bruce,* **right,** *to the Senate in 1874. Revels was the first African American seated in Congress. Bruce was the first to serve a full term.*

Representative Robert B. Elliot, **standing, left,** *delivers a speech in Congress in favor of passing the Civil Rights Act in 1874. The act passed in 1875.*

African Americans were a minority in the legislature of nearly every Southern state. There were no black governors, although African American Pinckney Benton Stewart Pinchback became lieutenant governor of Louisiana in 1871 and acting governor from December 1872 to January 1873. Throughout the South, the number of black men in office was small compared to the number of black citizens in the population.

African Americans made more progress with the Civil Rights Act of 1875. Although poorly enforced, the Civil Rights Act of 1875 outlawed discrimination in transportation, theaters, restaurants, hotels, and other public places.

The main goal of most African Americans, however, was to gain the full rights of citizenship and to enjoy equality with white citizens. Citizenship alone, they sensed, would protect freedom and make it meaningful. African Americans also reasoned that it would be important to have the right to buy and own land.

A SECOND BONDAGE

Of all the whole creation
* in the East or in the West,*
The Glorious Yankee nation
* is the greatest and the best.*
Come along! Come along!
* Don't be alarmed.*
Uncle Sam is rich enough
* to give you all a farm.*
                    —African American song

As early as 1865, African Americans had begun making their case for land ownership. To many black families, owning land was necessary to complete and maintain their independence. With land of their own, African Americans would not have to depend on white people to support themselves.

"Gib us our land and we take care of ourselves," said one former slave in Charleston, South Carolina. "But widout land," he added, "de ole masses [masters] can hire us or starve us, as dey please." Another slave described to his former mistress how he viewed the new order of things: "All de land belongs to de Yankees now, and dey gwine to divide it out 'mong de colored people. Besides, de kitchen ob de big house is my share. I help built hit."

As one Northern observer visiting South Carolina later wrote:

> The sole ambition of the freedman at the present time appears to be to become the owner of a little piece of land, there to erect a humble home, and to dwell in peace and security at his own free will and pleasure. If he wishes to cultivate the ground in cotton on his own account, to be able to do so without anyone to dictate to him hours or system of labor, if he wishes instead to plant corn or sweet potatoes—to be able to do that free from any outside control. . . . That is their idea, their desire and their hope.

Two Civil War policies gave many freedmen the hope that they would be given land. In 1864 the Union army had settled 75 former slaves on plantations once belonging to the family of Confederate president Jefferson Davis at Davis Bend, Mississippi. The so-called Davis Bend Relocation Plan was a great success. By 1865, 1,800 freedmen and their families were living on and working the land. President Andrew Johnson, however, returned the land to Davis's family members.

On January 16, 1865, General William T. Sherman had issued Field Order No. 15, setting aside land in South Carolina for former slaves. Each family received forty acres, and Sherman later loaned the families army mules to help with plowing. For many freedmen, the saying of "forty acres and a mule" expressed the belief that the federal government would provide for them the one thing that they most wished for and needed.

Providing land to all former slaves was not as easy as it may first have appeared, however. The Freedman's Bureau controlled approximately 800,000 acres that the federal government had taken from former Confederates. But the bureau was not willing to give the land among to freed slaves.

African Americans, meanwhile, argued passionately that they ought to receive land from the federal government. Land would help repay them for their years of unpaid slave labor. One former slave stated that "the land ought to belong to the man who could work it," while another argued that "the property which [the former masters] hold

African American settlers make their way to land granted to freedpersons through the Southern Homestead Act of 1866.

was nearly all earned by the sweat of our brows." Some freedmen refused to leave the plantations on which they lived, insisting that the property belonged to them. One freedman told his former master that he was "entitled to a part of the farm after all the work [the freedman] had done on it." Similarly, a Tennessee planter complained that his black foreman, Sidney, was not only claiming ownership of a portion of his land but had also moved his family into the slave owner's house.

MEETING THE CHALLENGE

In 1866 the federal government passed the Southern Homestead Act to help give farmland to more Southerners in Alabama, Arkansas, Florida, Louisiana, and Mississippi. Under the law, the head of any household, regardless of race, could apply for land. In writing the law, lawmakers also recognized that not just males headed households. The law also allowed women who could prove they were the head of a household to apply for land.

Whenever possible, African Americans throughout the South acquired land. During its first year, African Americans in Florida alone gained approximately 160,000 acres under the Southern Homestead Act. In Arkansas freedmen owned 116 of the 243 homesteads established. By 1874, eight years after passage of the Southern Homestead Act, former slaves in Georgia claimed more than 350,000 acres of land. Although most families never received "forty acres and a mule," more than forty thousand black families were eventually farming their own plots.

Since there wasn't enough available land for everyone, many black men and women could not take advantage of the Southern Homestead Act. Officials of the Freedmen's Bureau had a hard time explaining to

> "The slaves weren't expecting nothing. It got out somehow that they were going to give us forty acres and a mule. We all went up in town. They asked me who I belonged to and I told them my master was named Banner. One man said, 'Young man, I would go by my mama's name if I were you.' I told him my mother's name was Banner too. Then he opened a book and told me all the laws. He told me never to go by any name except Banner. That was all the mule they ever give me.
>
> "I started home a year after I got free and made a crop. I had my gear what I had saved on the plantation and went to town to get my mule but there wasn't any mule.

In this story, Freedman Henry Banner explains the problems many freedpersons faced when they tried to claim their "forty acres and a mule."

A group of freedpersons stands in line outside a state office, waiting to claim goods promised them by the U.S. government.

the former slaves why they could not have land. In one case, officials in Mississippi tried to give disappointed African Americans advice:

> The government owns no lands in this State. It therefore can give away none. Freedmen can obtain farms with the money which they have earned by their own labor. Everyone, therefore, shall work diligently, and carefully save his own wages, till he may be able to buy land and possess his own home.

One freedman took a unique approach to easing his disappointment. When he learned there was no land available, he lowered his expectations and told the agent for the Freedmen's Bureau that he would be content with only a single acre "ef you make it de acre dat Marsa's [Master's] house sets on."

BACK TO WORK

Since the federal government could not offer land to all the freedmen, many had to work for white employers. In some cases, black men and women had no choice but to return to the plantations on which they had toiled as slaves. They worked six days a week from sunrise to sunset, a schedule all too similar to slavery. Only their meager wages made their work different from slavery. Men earned between $9 and $15 a month (about $98 to $165 in modern money). Women earned between $5 and $10 (about $54 to $110 in modern money).

Another option for former slaves was to work as sharecroppers. Sharecroppers lived and farmed on white-owned land. Instead of wages, they were promised one-quarter to one-half of the cotton or corn crop they grew, which they could sell. In other cases, they were offered a percentage of the profit earned from their crops. White landowners usually provided housing and fuel. In some cases, they would provide food and medical care too. But they expected black families to repay the costs of all these services at the end of each year.

Many freedmen were reluctant to become sharecroppers, for fear of being enslaved all over again. In response to such fears, agents of the Freedmen's Bureau tried to be reassuring:

> Some of you have the absurd notion that if you put your hands to a contract you will somehow be made slaves. This is all nonsense, made up by some foolish or wicked person. There is no danger of this kind to fear.

But the fact of sharecropping was that many freedmen traded one kind of bondage for another.

A SECOND BONDAGE

Unable to keep up with expenses, sharecroppers and other black workers often found themselves heavily in debt to their employer. Former slave Sarah Wilson remembered how her family was forced to buy and sell all their goods at the store run by the plantation owner:

> De white man, he don't gib [us] no sho' 'nuf money. He jes gib [us] a . . . book, an' in dis here book dar's little pieces ob paper down at de plantation sto'e fer what [we] gwine git. But [we] can't go no whar else ter trade, only jes' on de plantation whar [we are] makin' de crop.

This system was supposed to provide sharecroppers and their families with everything they needed so that they would not have to go elsewhere to buy goods. And for many families, the plantation store was often filled with items they had gone without during slavery. Foods such as cheese, sugar, and sardines were much wanted. Other popular items included calico dresses, shoes, and even handkerchiefs.

But in most cases, the plantation owner charged unfairly, selling overpriced goods. This system almost always guaranteed that a sharecropper or laborer would soon be in debt to the store and the plantation owner. Many freedmen used all of their earnings just to pay back money they owed to their landlords or employers. They had been enslaved again, only this time by debt. As one South Carolina planter noted, "Heap of 'em round here, just works for their victuals [food] and clothes, like they always did. I reckon they'll all be back whar they was, in a few years."

To make matters worse, few white employers honored the terms of employment outlined in the labor contracts (written agreements between an employer and an employee) made with the freedmen. Employers continually broke contracts, even though they faced serious penalties from the Freedmen's Bureau for doing so. Frequently, white employers refused to pay the wages promised in the contract.

A sharecropper family rests in a cotton field. The sharecropping life was not much different from slavery.

Other times, they took advantage of their black workers' inability to read and write. On one plantation, for instance, the workers' contract stated that all laborers were to be paid one-third of seven-twelfths of the crop—seven thirty-sixths, a small amount. On another plantation, four freedmen discovered that they had signed labor contracts that said they would work for one-fifth of one-third (one-fifteenth) of the crop. "Contracts brought to me for approval," stated a Freedman's Bureau official in South Carolina, "contained all sorts of ludicrous provisions [ridiculous terms]. The idea seemed to be that if the laborer were not bound body and soul he would be of no use."

For many African Americans, working the fields was uncomfortably close to slavery. Labor contracts often contained the same language as the slave codes—harsh rules that had governed African Americans during slavery. Phrases such as "perfect obedience" or "prompt and faithful service" were common. Some landowners were more than happy to use the threat of violence to force both freedmen and their family members to work. And in almost all cases, the freedmen could do little about it legally. Yet African Americans found ways to fight back. Most simply refused to work. Others broke their contracts and left the job, risking arrest and jail. Many hoped to find better, or at least fairer, opportunities elsewhere.

IN SEARCH OF OTHER OPPORTUNITIES

Some freedmen wanted as little to do with farming as possible. Their years of toiling in the fields for the master had been more than enough. They moved to large Southern cities, such as Richmond, Virginia; New Orleans, Louisiana; or Jackson, Mississippi. Many of the jobs they found were higher paying than those on farms. Freedmen became factory workers, mechanics, or stevedores (dock workers). Occupations such as barbering drew other freedmen away from the fields. Women who came to the cities tended to find jobs inside the homes of white families as maids, cooks, or washerwomen. For the first time, freedmen and freedwomen had a choice as to where they wanted to work, and many made the most of it.

Some former slaves flourished in their own businesses. One group of Mississippi freedmen created a business selling their eggs and poultry to the highest bidder. Others who as slaves had been trained in a special skill, such as blacksmithing, carpentry, shoemaking, or brick masonry, started their own businesses.

Reconstruction paved the way for African Americans to become professionals, such as doctors and lawyers. But the wages earned by black lawyers, doctors, and professors fell far below those earned by white professionals. By far the largest group of African American

Henry Flipper, **left,** *and John H. Rock,* **right.** *Flipper was the first black graduate of West Point (a prestigious U.S. military school). Rock became one of the first African American attorneys. The men were among the small but growing number of black professionals during Reconstruction.*

professionals were church ministers. However, black ministers made little money and had to rely on other jobs to support themselves and their families.

Still for many former slaves, the ability to decide where to work and what kind of work they would do was a major step forward. But, as many discovered, this new freedom was not enough. They had learned that the Southern white community would do little to welcome them into white society. African Americans recognized that their true strength lay in numbers and in establishing their own institutions.

BLACK SPIRIT, BLACK MIND

We want power, it only comes through organization, and organization comes through unity. Our efforts must be one and inseparable, blended, tied, and bound together.

—Henry McNeal Turner, African American minister, 1866

African Americans worked against the effects of racism by developing their own social and political institutions. This was not an easy task. The scars of slavery were deep. Many African Americans still feared the angry power of their former white owners. Henry Turner, a former slave turned minister, later wrote:

> That old servile fear still twirls itself around the heartstrings [of African Americans], and fills with terror the entire soul at the white man's frown.... Oh, how the foul curse of slavery has blighted [spoiled] the natural greatness of my race!

For Turner and other African American leaders, one key to overcoming the past lay in the same thing that had carried them through the darkest of times of slavery: their faith.

"DE SPIRIT MOVES ME EVERY DAY"

Organized religion was nothing new to the newly freed men and women. As slaves, many had spent their Sundays attending services at their master's church. They had not been part of the actual congregation but were forced to sit in the upper lofts where they could watch—not participate—in the white services. Sometimes with the master's permission, and often without it, African American slaves met to worship together in their own quarters. Their religion combined elements of old and new. It drew as much from the religions of their African ancestors as from the Christian religion of their owners.

With the Emancipation Proclamation and the end of the Civil War, African Americans were free to worship in their own churches.

A group of freedpersons gather at their church. Churches were community centers for freedpersons, serving as places to worship, to attend school, and to organize and discuss political matters.

For many former slaves, the freedom to worship was as exhilarating as emancipation itself. As one freedman exclaimed, "Praise God for this day of liberty to worship God!" By the time of Reconstruction, many African Americans had organized their own churches. These churches became the very first social institutions controlled by African Americans. They were important both symbolically and physically. They offered a sense of identity and unity that nourished the growth of a culture of free African Americans. At the same time, they offered African Americans a place where community members could come together to worship and to interact with each other. The church served a variety of functions. It could house a school, social events, and political gatherings.

Churches also acted as charitable organizations, helping families and individuals during times of illness and death. The churches also sheltered African Americans against white racism and violence. In time, the church became the place to settle disputes between church members without having to go to the white-controlled courts.

In operating their churches, African Americans learned to master self-government by coping with problems of finance, planning, cooperation, and discipline. Black church members worked together to raise money for buildings, to pay ministers, and to offer assistance to those in need. They planned special events and provided advice to community members. And they often developed ways to strengthen their rights, such as teaching African Americans how to vote. These experiences taught many African Americans how to manage their lives as individuals and as a free community.

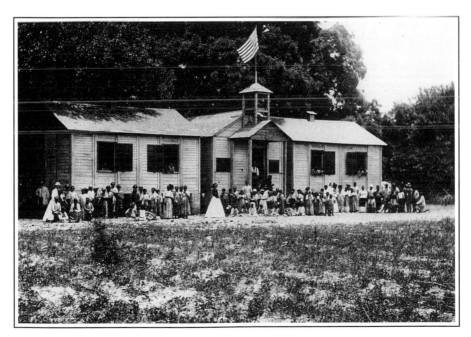

Students and teachers gather outside a freedpersons' church school. Through churches, freedpersons taught skills such as reading.

Throughout Reconstruction, independent black churches appeared everywhere in the South. As black churchgoers stopped attending white churches, attendance at black churches grew all across the South. Membership in the Baptist Church also rose from 150,000 in 1850 to approximately 500,000 by 1870. In older, more established black churches, such as the African Methodist Episcopal (AME) Church, membership increased dramatically, rising from 75,000 members in 1856 to more than 200,000 by 1876.

Along with the growth of black churches came the creation of thousands of societies and clubs. These included workers associations, volunteer fire companies, and trade associations for black business owners. Mutual aid and burial societies also formed. Members paid dues to these organizations to make sure that their families would be taken care of in case of sickness or death. By 1870 more than two

Freedpersons run a ration service, offering food to those in need, including whites, in the rural South.

hundred such organizations existed in Memphis, Tennessee, alone. Richmond, Virginia, boasted more than four hundred similar groups.

These organizations offered black men and women additional opportunities to meet, socialize and, in some cases, organize in support of other causes important to them. Black groups in Nashville, Jackson, and New Orleans raised money to establish orphanages, soup kitchens, and employment agencies for black people throughout the South. One black mutual aid society in West Virginia even contributed money to help poor white families in the area.

For many African Americans, the chance to worship and meet freely matched the intense desire to learn to read the Bible. The hope of reading the word of God for themselves led many African Americans to pursue an education, which tradition and law had previously denied them. But for many African Americans, learning to read meant something more. It was a ticket to bettering themselves and the community.

READIN', 'RITIN', AND RECONSTRUCTION

As a slave, Charles Whiteside never forgot the words of his master when he gained his freedom. "Charles, you is a free man they [say], but Ah tells you now, you is still a slave and if you lives to be a hundred, you'll STILL be a slave, cause you got no education, and education is what makes a man free!" For Charles and thousands of newly freed slaves, this piece of advice only made them more determined to take advantage of a major new opportunity —the opportunity to learn to read and write.

Newly freed men and women knew firsthand what happened to those who did not know how to read and write. Illiterate black workers could count on being cheated by their white employers because they could not read a contract or do the necessary mathematics to calculate wages owed to them. Reading a newspaper was out of the question. And many freedmen soon learned that if they could not read or write, they could not vote. New tests at the polls,

Freedpersons learned valuable trades by taking classes offered by the Freedman's Bureau. The freedwomen above are learning to be seamstresses.

or places of voting, required blacks to prove they could read. For many newly freed slaves, knowledge truly was power. And the more they could learn, the more they could be in charge of their own lives. As one freed slave in South Carolina exclaimed to a white teacher, "My Lord, ma'am, what a great thing larning is! White folks can do what they likes, for the[y] know so much more'na we."

The Freedmen's Bureau was highly successful in creating schools for African Americans. The bureau established day·schools for children, night schools for adults, industrial training schools for those who wished to learn a trade, and even Sunday schools. With the help of charitable and religious organizations in the North, the bureau also founded black colleges for those who wished to pursue higher education or gain professional training. The colleges founded during this period include: Howard University in Washington, D.C., Hampton Institute, in Hampton, Virginia, Atlanta University, in

Atlanta, Georgia, Fisk University, in Nashville, Tennessee, and Storer College, in Harpers Ferry, West Virginia.

Hundreds of white teachers and black teachers and missionaries from the North helped the bureau. Many white missionaries and teachers came to the South with the lofty goal of aiding the newly freed slaves. But the reality of working so closely with African Americans brought mixed feelings about their new students.

Lydia Maria Child, a well-known abolitionist, noted of her friends teaching in the South, "I doubt whether we *can* treat our colored brethren *exactly* as we would if they were white, though it would be desirable to do so." Another teacher writing from North Carolina bluntly stated, "It is *one* thing to [sit] in one's office or drawing room and weave fine spun theories in regard to the Negro character, but it is quite another to come into actual contact with him. I fail to see the beauties and excellencies [of black people] that some do." Such racist attitudes often caused African American communities to seek out African American teachers whenever possible.

The Old Main Building of Howard University, in Washington, D.C. The Freedman's Bureau established this college for freedpersons in 1866 and named it after Major General Oliver O. Howard, bureau commissioner.

A DREAM REALIZED

African Americans set about helping to establish schoolhouses in their communities as soon as they could. They transformed churches, private homes, empty warehouses and hotels, and abandoned pool halls into classrooms that rapidly filled with students. In Richmond, Virginia, more than 1,000 black children and 75 adults attended classes that area churches sponsored with help from a white organization called the American Missionary Association. Even former slave markets, the places where slaves had been bought and sold, became places of learning. In Savannah, Georgia, the Bryant Slave Market, with its iron-grated windows and handcuffs and whips, became a school. In New Orleans, a pen that once held slaves to be sold was named the Frederick Douglass School.

African Americans did all they could to attract the best teachers to their communities. Poverty, though, proved a barrier. Teachers in black schools usually received small salaries compared to educators who taught elsewhere. African American parents tried to make up for the low pay by opening their homes to teachers and providing them with room and board at little or no cost. But scraping together funds to pay a teacher's salary was not only a burden, it was also an opportunity. As one freedman explained, it was a chance to demonstrate "the first proof of their *independence*."

With a shortage of qualified teachers in many black communities, teachers in black schools were often not as well prepared as those who taught in white schools. Many black teachers were aware of their shortcomings. One reported to the Freedmen's Bureau, "I have no education only what I gave myself by chance. . . ." Another explained, "I never had the chance of goen to school for I was a slave until freedom. . . . I am the only teacher because we can not doe better now."

Many African Americans regarded education for their children with the utmost seriousness. They considered education among the greatest benefits of freedom. It was common for workers to demand that employers establish schoolhouses for their children. A Freedmen's Bureau official in Mississippi recalled that when he had informed a gathering of 3,000 freed slaves that they "were to have the advantages of schools and education, their joy knew no bounds. They fairly jumped and shouted in gladness."

Education was thought to be so important in many black sharecropping families that parents made the difficult decision to send their children to school. If children were at school, they would not be able to work in the fields and earn money for their families. But many black families were more than willing to make the sacrifice. As one Louisiana freedman explained, "Leaving learning to your children was better than leaving them a fortune because if you left them even five hundred dollars, some man having more education than they had would come along and cheat them out of it all."

These African American children are dressed for school. Deprived of education for centuries, freedpersons valued education above much else.

A young freedwoman eagerly reads a book while other children play.

The quest for knowledge also extended outside the classroom. Black schoolchildren helped their parents learn the alphabet. The parents haltingly studied their children's grammar and reading lessons or grappled with the morning newspaper during their lunch hour. Then, too, there were the makeshift "wayside schools," of which an official for the Freedmen's Bureau has left a memorable description:

> A negro riding on a loaded wagon, or . . . waiting for a train, or [sitting] by the cabin door, is often seen, book in hand [seeking the basics] of knowledge. A group on the platform of a depot, after carefully [acquiring] an old spelling book, [forms] into a class.

Black education throughout the South was so successful that by 1867 schools had been set up in even the most remote counties of the former Confederate states. By 1870 more than 4,000 schools for black people were opened, with more than 9,000 teachers serving nearly 250,000 students. By 1870, only five years after the end of the

Civil War, approximately one-fourth of African American school-children in the South were attending school. At the same time, African Americans had raised more than $1 million to bring education to former slaves.

GETTING RID OF "NUISANCES"

Not everyone was pleased with educating the freedmen. Some white Southerners argued about the foolishness of educating former slaves. Said one white woman to a teacher, "I do assure you, you might as well teach your horse or mule to read, as to teach these [black people]. They *can't* learn." Slaves who worked as field hands were thought to be especially unable to learn, as the same woman pointed out, "You can't *learn* them to come out of the rain."

What seemed to alarm most white Southerners, though, was how education would lead the black community toward equality with whites. One white teacher wrote:

> Suppose our educational schemes succeeded, suppose we elevate [the black man] as a race until he has the instincts and drives of a white man. . . . Being trained for office he will demand office. Being taught as a Negro child the same things in the same way as the white child, when he becomes a Negro man he will want the same things and demand them the same way as a white man.

While some white people debated the question in their parlors, others used fear to try to stop black people from forming schools. Setting fire to schools was a common form of intimidation. In one small town in Mississippi, African Americans were told that if they built a schoolhouse, the structure would be burned to the ground. Said one Virginia freedman, "Down in my neighborhood they [African Americans] are afraid to be caught with a book."

Burning down schools was only one tool used by Southern whites to make their point. Visiting teachers from the North often could find no place to live or were turned away from local stores. One female teacher in Louisiana was threatened with a public hanging, while another teacher was "accidentally" shot. Even in areas where the freedmen's schools were tolerated, white teachers were shunned by white Southerners. Many teachers and superintendents of these schools turned to nearby federal troops for protection at home and in schoolhouses.

CULTURAL TENSIONS

As former slaves worked together to strengthen their communities, they struggled with their identity as black Americans. For some the question was not so much how to embrace their black heritage but how to distance themselves from it. To do this, they adopted the fashions, manners, speech, and even skin color of white people. Many hoped they would be more fully accepted into American society.

During Reconstruction many black newspapers began to advertise skin creams, hair relaxers, and other cosmetics that promised to enable black men and women to "blend in" with white society.

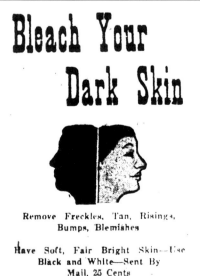

This newspaper advertisement from Reconstruction offers a cream that lightens skin. The message to blacks and whites alike was clear: light or white skin is best.

Chastellar's White Liquid Enamel vowed to lighten the complexion, giving black women the "beauty which was once so precious and rare." Other advertisements promised black women that, with regular use, Chastellar's White Liquid Enamel would give them the "famed beauty of the Caucasians."

Many African Americans spent money they did not have to imitate the appearance of those in white society. Some black women spent their hard-earned money on expensive dresses, shoes, and jewelry that they had seen white women wear. In the process, they plunged themselves deeper into debt in an effort not to look poor. Yet they felt they had the right to look their best. Others were concerned that black people were too busy trying to look and act like white people. One black Louisiana newspaper wrote:

> Because we had to put up with a home-spun suit before emancipation we are determined to wear a silk one now no matter at what cost to our stomachs or our landlords. . . . Yet it is a painful fact that we will spend more time and money to appear what we are not, than it would to be what we pretend to be.

How could black people claim their rights and privileges as Americans without sacrificing their culture, heritage, and identity—without, that is, becoming white? The African American scholar and activist W. E. B. Du Bois advised that the black man:

> not bleach his Negro soul in a flood of white Americanism, for he knows that Negro blood has a message for the world. He simply wishes to make it possible for a man to be both a Negro and an American, without being cursed and spit upon by his fellows, without having the doors of Opportunity closed roughly in his face.

A NEW WAR

Our only crime is that we are negroes.
—unidentified African American newspaper reporter, 1874

With defeat and emancipation, Southern society had been turned upside down. Many white Southerners were left confused, unsure, and angry. Alarmed whites throughout the South complained, feeling that the newly freed slaves were flaunting (showing off) their new freedoms and status.

African Americans found small and large ways to express their new freedom. Many who had always stepped aside to let white people pass when meeting on roads or walkways challenged both the law and the power of their former masters by not moving aside. They chose their own work and sent their children to school. Even those African Americans who remained as workers on the plantations often carried out their chores in an atmosphere of conflict and confrontation. On the Bradford plantation in Florida, for example, the family cook informed

Mrs. Bradford that if she wanted dinner, "she kin cook it herself." That remark later prompted the Bradfords' daughter, Susan, to note in her diary that the blacks "are not ours any longer."

Former slaveholders wondered, although seldom aloud, how they would survive without their slaves. Who would cultivate their land, care for their houses, cook their meals, raise their children, and satisfy their demands? Desolation, outrage, and sorrow spread. The slaves had left, observed a sad Emily Caroline Douglas of Louisiana, "without even a goodbye." Her words echoed throughout the South.

THE BLACK CODES

Many white Southerners were determined to reestablish the old social system of the South, in which African Americans would be prevented from enjoying equal rights. As early as 1865 and 1866, legislatures in all Southern states except North Carolina had begun to enact "Black Codes." These were laws designed to control African Americans and restrict their rights as citizens of the United States.

An abandoned plantation house in the late 1860s. The freeing of the slaves meant many former slaveholders were forced to run their plantations without free labor. Many plantations, like this one, crumbled.

Although the Black Codes varied from state to state, most of them included racial segregation, or separation, in public places and the prohibition of interracial marriage. The Black Codes also prevented African Americans from serving on juries or testifying against white people in court. In some states, such as Mississippi, these laws also brought back some of the harsh slave codes. The Mississippi code declared that all laws describing punishments for "slaves, free negroes, or mulattoes [people of mixed race] are hereby reenacted, and decreed to be in full force against all freedmen, free negroes, and mulattoes."

The laws in general forbade African Americans from seeking employment other than working for white landowners. In South Carolina, the Black Codes made it illegal for African Americans to purchase or own land in cities and forced them to pay a tax of from $10 to $100 to enter an occupation other than farming or domestic service.

At first, freedmen, like the men above, had the same right to serve on juries as did white men. Black Codes, however, took away this right.

Under the Black Codes, many freedmen had to sign unfair and harsh labor contracts.

African Americans were also prohibited from leaving plantations where they worked and from inviting guests without permission.

In Mississippi the codes prevented black people from buying or renting farmland and required them to sign a yearly labor contract with a white employer. If African Americans could not prove they had jobs, white police officers could fine or jail them. If unable to pay their fine, they could be forced to work for a white landowner. Laws also allowed the state to send black children to work for white employers if the children's parents could not support them or were "not teaching them habits of industry and honesty; or are persons of notoriously bad character."

The Black Codes revealed what life would be like for African Americans in the post-Civil War South if power were left entirely in the hands of conservative white Southerners. As W. E. B. Du Bois observed, the Black Codes represented "what the South proposed to do to the emancipated Negro, unless restrained by the nation."

Black congressman Josiah Walls warned that the Black Codes revealed what Southern Democrats would do "if they should ever again obtain control of this Government." White leaders intended these laws to keep African Americans as a rural, laboring people without property—slaves in everything but name.

"RIGHT WILL PREVAIL"

With the adoption of the Black Codes, African Americans found themselves in nearly the same position they had held as slaves. The Black Codes had replaced the laws that had recognized their citizenship and their rights. Some freedmen protested the Black Codes. A letter to the governor of Mississippi from a group of freedmen asserted: "Mississippi has abolished slavery. Does she [the state] mean it or is it a policy for the present?"

Politician Josiah Walls was outspoken about the injustice of the Black Codes while serving in Florida's state government and in the U.S. House of Representatives. Walls's opponents worked hard to remove him from government, succeeding in 1874.

Freedpersons spoke out against the Black Codes in any way they could, such as by writing newspaper articles like the one at right.

> **WIPE OUT THE "BLACK LAWS."**
>
> We contend for rights involved in the exercise of personal liberty. Now what are personal rights, but human rights, the rights of all men, and who dares challenge them? If, as a citizen under the General Government, man enjoys privileges sanctioned by constitutional guarantees, then, as a citizen, he must oppose and fight down every unnatural restriction imposed upon those privileges. No matter how difficult or embarrassing the undertaking, we must contend for every inch of the ground and surrender nothing of the common allotment. Experience has shown that, as with England's boasted Normans and as with the fathers of this republic, they won nothing and secured nothing except by persistent and unceasing endeavor to rise to a just and equal plane with those who represent authority. Regardless of color or previous condition of servitude, the American citizen

Most African Americans realized that their protests would have little effect on the situation. At the same time, as one writer for an African American newspaper stated, they believed that "the right will prevail [win] and truth [will] triumph in the end." Eventually, the federal government stepped in and outlawed the Black Codes in several states. Some Southern state legislatures abolished the harshest laws on their own. But while the codes were considered "dead," the white fury that had created them was very much alive.

TERROR IN WHITE

With the failure of the Black Codes, white Southerners tried to limit the freedom and power of African Americans through intimidation, violence, and terror. The largest number of violent acts against black people came when African Americans tried to assert their rights. Freedmen and freed-women were assaulted and, in some cases, murdered for not meeting their employers' demands, for trying to buy or rent land, or simply for trying to leave the plantations on which they had once been enslaved. One Tennessee newspaper reported that white "regulators" were "riding about whipping, maiming and killing all the negroes who do not obey the orders of their former masters, just as if slavery existed."

One of the greatest threats to African Americans was a new organization determined to threaten them and their white supporters: the Ku Klux Klan. Organized in 1866 in Pulaski, Tennessee, the Klan set out to restore white supremacy (absolute white control) in the South. While at first nothing more than a social group, the Klan's activities soon became threatening. Klansmen rode about the Southern countryside wearing white masks and robes, issuing threats, harassing

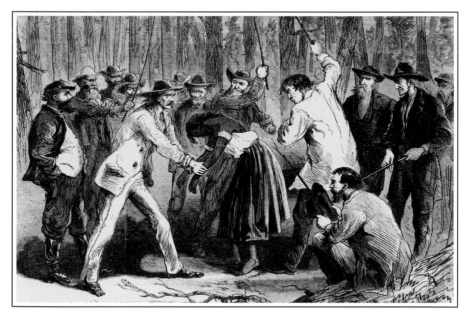

A group of white men whip a freedwoman in 1867 to remind her of "her place" in white society. Some whites used physical violence to discourage African Americans from asserting their civil rights.

Members of the Ku Klux Klan used secrecy and intimidation to preserve white power in the South.

black citizens and, on occasion, engaging in destruction, violence, and murder. The Klan and similar groups, such as the Knights of the White Camellia and the White League, according to one later historian of the period, "whipped, shot, hanged, robbed, raped, and otherwise outraged Negroes and Republicans across the South in the name of preserving white civilization."

"DEM KLUXERS"

At first, the aim of the organization was to discourage black men from voting and to prevent African Americans from holding political office. F. H. Brown, the son of a sharecropper, remembered how the Klan would visit his father's farm, warning him not to vote on Election Day. Other tactics included beating or whipping freedmen to keep them from going to the polls and even getting them too drunk to vote. The Klan also targeted white citizens thought to be too friendly or helpful toward African Americans, particularly around election time.

But this was only the beginning. The freeing of the slaves and their new status as full citizens enraged many white citizens during Reconstruction. The Southern defeat in the Civil War had humiliated white Southerners and destroyed their social system. They looked for ways to express their anger and their desire to return to the old way of life.

At first, Klan members tried to intimidate African Americans verbally, often visiting the homes of black citizens at night. Former slave Anderson Furr recalled one evening visit to his home: "One of dem Kluxers come to our house . . . and talked to us 'bout how us ought to act. . . . Us allus thought it was our old master, all dressed up in dem white robes, wid his face kivvered up and a-talking in a strange, put-on . . . voice."

When verbal intimidation did not work, the Klan turned to more violent methods to frighten former slaves into submissiveness.

Kluxers raid an African American home. The Klan used violence and murder to achieve its goals.

A Freedman's Bureau school burns in the late 1860s. Klansmen and other citizens targeted African American schools to keep freedpersons from going to school.

Brawley Gilmore remembered how the Klan would kidnap freedmen, take them to a nearby bridge, shoot them, and then throw their bodies in the water. Some freedmen, such as John McDonald, hid in the woods, even though there were panthers and rattlesnakes living there. As McDonald later stated, "We was terrible [scared] but we was more [scared] of de Ku Klux Klan."

Pierce Harper, a former slave, recalled that one of the worse things about Klan members was their hidden identities:

> Dey wore dem long sheets, an' you couldn't tell who dey was. Dey even covered their horses up. . . . Men you thought was your friends was the Ku Kluxes. You deal wit 'em in de stores in de daytime, an' at night dey come out to your house an' kill you.

By using threats, intimidation, and physical violence, some white Southerners hoped to regain political and social control of their states.

In many instances, the Klan succeeded. In 1869 in North Carolina, where the Republicans had won major victories, the Klan whipped and beat African American officeholders. The following year, with the Klan's help at election time, the Democrats won control of the legislature.

STRIKING BACK

The U.S. Congress struck back at the Klan with three enforcement acts passed in 1870 and 1871. The first of these laws made it a federal crime to interfere with any citizen's right to vote. The second placed the election of congressmen under the supervision of federal election officials and marshals. The third, the so-called Ku Klux Klan Act, made it illegal to engage in conspiracies, to wear disguises, and to resist, threaten, or in any way intimidate officials of the courts or the government.

African American legislators during Reconstruction, including Revels, front left, Walls, front center, and Elliot, front right, helped pass legislation that outlawed the terrorist activity of the Ku Klux Klan.

Federal laws weakened the Klan, but other societies such as the Mississippi Rifle Club and the South Carolina Red Shirts continued to harass African Americans and white Republicans. Their activities allowed conservative white leaders gradually to regain control of government and society in one Southern state after another.

The use of intimidation, violence, and the Black Codes greatly weakened Republican control of Southern states. Republicans fell out of power in Virginia and Tennessee in 1869 and in Georgia and North Carolina in 1870. The "Old North State" (North Carolina) had a Republican governor until 1876. The Republicans held on to power longer in the states farther south, which had larger black populations than those in the upper South. In the elections of 1876, however, conservative white voters successfully dismissed the Republicans from office in South Carolina, Louisiana, and Florida, the three remaining states where they had controlled state government. The last Republican governor of South Carolina summed up the situation, explaining to the former abolitionist William Lloyd Garrison that "the uneducated negro was too weak, no matter what his numbers, to cope with the whites."

REDEMPTION AND REJECTION

The slave went free; stood a brief moment in the sun; then moved back toward slavery.
　　　　　　　—W. E. B.
　　　　Du Bois (right), 1875

Northern support for Reconstruction began to lessen with the Panic of 1873, a severe economic depression that spread throughout the country. Economic hard times distracted Northerners and the federal government from the problems of the former slaves and made Reconstruction programs seem like an expensive luxury. Without the support of the federal government, Reconstruction collapsed.

THE COMPROMISE OF 1877
The presidential election of 1876 marked the formal end of Reconstruction. Both Rutherford B. Hayes, the Republican candidate, and Democrat Samuel J. Tilden favored restoring conservative leaders in the South. They both promised to reestablish Southern governments under

the control of wealthy white landowners. On Election Day, Tilden was just short of the necessary majority of votes to become president. Congress set up a special commission, or group, of legislators to decide the election. The commission decided Hayes won the election, but Democratic leaders said they would not approve the decision.

The Democrats and Republicans in Congress came up with a compromise, known as the Compromise of 1877. Republicans agreed that if the Democrats accepted the commission's decision, Hayes would withdraw federal troops from certain Southern states where the troops remained. And he would let the Reconstruction governments in those states collapse. In exchange, the Democrats promised to accept the Reconstruction amendments to the Constitution (the thirteenth, the fourteenth, and the fifteenth, which granted African American men the vote). On March 2, 1877, the House of Representatives declared Hayes to be the president of the United States.

Democratic candidate Samuel Tilden, **far left,** *and Republican candidate Rutherford B. Hayes,* **far right.** *A deal in Congress made Hayes president of the United States and marked the end of Reconstruction.*

Southerners reasoned that the Compromise of 1877 at last "redeemed" (freed) the South from Republican rule and restored conservative Democrats to power in state government. In April President Hayes fulfilled his part of the agreement by withdrawing federal troops from the South. During the next thirty years, the rights that African Americans had struggled to win were taken from them one by one.

A RIGHT IS LOST

Some white leaders wanted to put an end to black citizens' right to vote. But the Fifteenth Amendment made it impossible to outlaw the black vote, so white Southerners came up with other, less direct ways to keep black men from voting. They created a poll tax, a fee that most African Americans were required but could not afford to

With federal troops gone from the South, some Southerners weren't afraid to openly threaten African Americans to keep them from voting.

Senator Henry Cabot Lodge introduced a bill in the U.S. Senate in 1890 that called for an examination of Southern voting laws. The bill was defeated.

pay at the voting place. They also established new literacy (reading and writing) tests that most African Americans could not pass.

The new voting restrictions were very effective in discouraging blacks from voting. In 1896, 130,000 black men registered to vote in Louisiana. By 1900 that number had fallen to 5,320. In 1900, Alabama had 121,259 literate black men over the age of twenty-one, all of whom ought to have been eligible to vote. Only 3,742 were registered.

The federal government did little to improve the situation. In 1890 the U.S. Senate defeated a bill sponsored by Senator Henry Cabot Lodge of Massachusetts. The bill would have allowed federal officers to reexamine the rules for voting in Southern states. Lodge's bill was the last major attempt to protect black voters until Congress passed the Voting Rights Act in 1965.

THE SEGREGATED SOUTH

The U.S. Supreme Court also played an important role in weakening the rights of African Americans. In 1883 the Court ruled that the Civil Rights Act of 1875 was unconstitutional. The court declared that no law could prevent private organizations, companies, or individuals from discriminating against African Americans. For this reason, railroad and streetcar companies, restaurants, hotels, theaters, private clubs, hospitals, and other places could legally refused to serve black citizens if they wished.

In 1896 the Supreme Court ruled on another case known as *Plessy v. Ferguson.* In this ruling, the Court stated that separate seating arrangements on public transportation did not take away the constitutional rights of African Americans. In other words, the Court declared that segregation was not illegal. The one voice of disagreement came from Justice John Marshall Harlan, a former slaveholder from Kentucky. "In my opinion," Harlan wrote, "the judgment this day rendered will, in time, prove to be quite . . . pernicious [evil]."

An angry white passenger orders a freedman out of a white train car in the 1890s. The Supreme Court's decision in the **Plessy v. Ferguson** *case in 1896 legalized segregation in the United States. The Court's ruling created "separate but equal" facilities for whites and people of color. These separate facilities, however, were seldom equal.*

Segregation led to increased violence toward African Americans in the South and the rest of the country. In this photo, a freedman is about to be lynched (hanged).

The ruling, Harlan predicted, would "stimulate aggressions, more or less brutal, upon the admitted rights of colored citizens."

Harlan's prediction came true. Soon segregation extended to every aspect of life for African Americans, from public places (such as restaurants and hotels) to recreation and sports to health care and employment. At the end of the nineteenth century, in *Cumming v. County Board of Education,* the Supreme Court also ruled that separate schools for white children and black children were constitutional.

The violence that Justice Harlan had warned of became a reality as well. Between 1890 and 1899, the number of black lynchings (the murdering of African Americans by white mobs) in the United States averaged 187.5 per year. Eighty-two percent of them took place in the South.

A PROMISE UNFULFILLED

With the help of the federal government and some state governments, African Americans had gained some political power during Reconstruction. Within a few years of emancipation, the freed slaves had won important rights, which opened doors of opportunity that were never again completely closed. Yet this revolutionary experiment in freedom and democracy proved impossible to sustain.

Few white citizens, in the North or South, ever fully accepted the idea of equality for former slaves. The dreams of equality held by many black Americans remained unfulfilled. At the dawn of the twentieth century, most African Americans in the South were struggling as sharecroppers or plantation workers. Few owned land or earned enough money to buy land in the future. They remained poor and without property, both dependent on and at the mercy of white citizens.

Former Confederate general Robert V. Richardson, treasurer of the American Cotton Planters' Association, predicted the limits of Reconstruction when he wrote in December 1865: "The emancipated slaves own nothing, because nothing but freedom has been given to them." Like many of his contemporaries, whether congressmen or freedmen, General Richardson knew that freedom without equal rights and opportunities was not nearly enough. It put African Americans into mainstream society poor, uneducated, and disadvantaged in many ways. To mean anything, freedom had to mean more than only the end of slavery.

HOW FREE IS FREE?

Yet, whatever its limitations, freedom was more than nothing—much more. The failure of Reconstruction, the survival of the plantation system, and the ongoing exploitation of African Americans did not wipe out the power of emancipation. For African Americans, the end of slavery always and forever marked a major turning point. In 1883 the Reverend E. P. Holmes of Georgia, a former house slave, testified before a Senate committee. In his speech, he made plain the importance that freedom had for black people, no matter the hardships. "Most anyone ought to know that a man is better off free than as a slave," Holmes declared, "even if he did not have anything. I would rather be free and have my liberty. I fared just as well as any white child could have fared when I was a slave, and yet I would not give up my freedom." During the next century, the promise of Reconstruction would not be forgotten as African Americans fought for their rights in a courageous effort to "cross on over to freedom's land" at last.

An African American song of Reconstruction, "Slavery Passed Away," expresses the joy of freedom.

TIMELINE

1860 Abraham Lincoln is elected president.
South Carolina secedes from the Union on December 20, 1860.

1861 Mississippi, Florida, Alabama, Georgia, Louisiana, and Texas secede from the Union before the start of the Civil War.
The Civil War begins on April 12.
Virginia, Arkansas, North Carolina, and Tennessee secede from the Union.

1863 Abraham Lincoln puts the Emancipation Proclamation into effect on January 1.
Lincoln announces his plans in December for Reconstruction.

1864 Lincoln vetoes a congressional plan for Reconstruction.

1865 Congress approves the Thirteenth Amendment, adopted into the Constitution in December, which abolishes slavery throughout the United States.
Congress creates the Freedman's Bureau in March.
The Civil War ends on April 9 when General Robert E. Lee surrenders to General Ulysses S. Grant.
Abraham Lincoln is assassinated in April, and Andrew Johnson becomes president.
Johnson carries out his plans for Reconstruction.

1866 Republicans in Congress work to pass the Freedman's Bureau Act (which extends the existence of the Bureau) and the Civil Rights Act of 1866 (which bases citizenship on country of birth, rather than race, and provides for equal protection under the law for all citizens).

1867 Radical Republicans in Congress work to pass three Reconstruction Acts. These laws divide the former Confederate states into five military districts and give military governors power to run state constitutional conventions and remove state officials from office.

1868 The House of Representatives impeaches President Andrew Johnson, but Johnson is not convicted and remains in office.
The Fourteenth Amendment, adopted into the Constitution in July, guarantees the rights of citizenship and equal protection under the law to all Americans, regardless of race.
Ulysses S. Grant is elected president of the United States in November.

1870 The Fifteenth Amendment, adopted into the Constitution in March, grants voting rights to male U.S. citizens, regardless of race, color, or previous condition of servitude.
Congress passes the first of three Enforcement Acts to protect the rights of African Americans.

1871 Congress passes the second and third Enforcement Acts.

1873 An economic depression, known as the Panic of 1873, sweeps the nation.

1875 Congress passes the Civil Rights Act of 1875 in March, outlawing discrimination in transportation, theaters, restaurants, hotels, and other places of public accommodation.

1877 After a close presidential election, Democrats and Republicans in Congress agree on the Compromise of 1877. The House of Representatives chooses Republican Rutherford B. Hayes as president over Democrat Samuel J. Tilden. Reconstruction officially ends.

1883 The Supreme Court rules against the Civil Rights Act of 1875.

1896 In *Plessy v. Ferguson,* the Supreme Court rules that segregation is legal.

1899 In *Cumming v. County Board of Education,* the Supreme Court rules that separate schools for white children and black children are constitutional.

EMANCIPATION PROCLAMATION, 1863

Issued by President Abraham Lincoln on January 1, 1863, this document declared that all slaves living in the Confederate states must be freed. The proclamation did not actually free any slaves, but it made the fight against slavery a major focus of the Civil War. True freedom did not come to African Americans until the North won the war in 1865.

By the President of the United States of America:
A Proclamation.

WHEREAS, ON THE TWENTY SECOND DAY OF SEPTEMBER, in the year of our Lord one thousand eight hundred and sixty[-]two, a proclamation was issued by the President of the United States, containing, among other things, the following, to wit:

"That on the first day of January, in the year of our Lord one thousand eight hundred and sixty-three, all persons held as slaves within any State or designated part of a State, the people whereof shall then be in rebellion against the United States, shall be then, thenceforward, and forever free; and the Executive Government of the United States, including the military and naval authority thereof, will recognize and maintain the freedom of such persons, and will do no act or acts to repress such persons, or any of them, in any efforts they may make for their actual freedom.

"That the Executive will, on the first day of January aforesaid, by proclamation, designate the States and parts of States, if any, in which the people thereof, respectively, shall then be in rebellion against the United States; and the fact that any State, or the people thereof, shall on that day be, in good faith, represented in the Congress of the United States by members chosen thereto at elections wherein a majority of the qualified voters of such State shall have participated, shall, in the absence of strong countervailing testimony, be deemed conclusive evidence that such State, and the people thereof, are not then in rebellion against the United States."

Now, therefore I, Abraham Lincoln, President of the United States, by virtue of the power in me vested as Commander-in-Chief, of the Army and Navy of the United States in time of actual armed rebellion against the authority and government of the United States, and as a fit and necessary war measure for suppress-

President Abraham Lincoln

ing said rebellion, do, on this first day of January, in the year of our Lord one thousand eight hundred and sixty three, and in accordance with my purpose so to do publicly proclaimed for the full period of one hundred days, from the day first above mentioned, order and designate as the States and parts of States wherein the people thereof respectively, are this day in rebellion against the United States, the following, to wit:

Arkansas, Texas, Louisiana, (except the Parishes of St. Bernard, Plaquemines, Jefferson, St. Johns, St. Charles, St. James[,] Ascension, Assumption, Terrebonne, Lafourche, St. Mary, St. Martin, and Orleans, including the City of New Orleans) Mississippi, Alabama, Florida, Georgia, South Carolina, North Carolina, and Virginia, (except the forty-eight counties designated as West Virginia, and also the counties of Berkley, Accomac, Northampton, Elizabeth-City, York, Princess Ann, and Norfolk, including the cities of Norfolk and Portsmouth[])], and which excepted parts, are for the present, left precisely as if this proclamation were not issued.

And by virtue of the power, and for the purpose aforesaid, I do order and declare that all persons held as slaves within said designated States, and parts of States, are, and henceforward shall be free; and that the Executive government of the United States, including the military and naval authorities thereof, will recognize and maintain the freedom of said persons.

And I hereby enjoin upon the people so declared to be free to abstain from all violence, unless in necessary self-defense; and I recommend to them that, in all cases when allowed, they labor faithfully for reasonable wages.

And I further declare and make known, that such persons of suitable condition, will be received into the armed service of the United States to garrison forts, positions, stations, and other places, and to man vessels of all sorts in said service.

And upon this act, sincerely believed to be an act of justice, warranted by the Constitution, upon military necessity, I invoke the considerate judgment of mankind, and the gracious favor of Almighty God.

In witness whereof, I have hereunto set my hand and caused the seal of the United States to be affixed.

Done at the City of Washington, this first day of January, in the year of our Lord one thousand eight hundred and sixty three, and of the Independence of the United States of America the eighty-seventh.

By the President: ABRAHAM LINCOLN

WILLIAM H. SEWARD, Secretary of State

THE FOURTEENTH AMENDMENT
TO THE CONSTITUTION OF THE UNITED STATES, 1868

This amendment was added to the U.S. Constitution in 1868 in order to protect the rights of newly freed slaves. It guarantees equal protection under the law to all U.S. citizens regardless of race.

Section 1. All persons born or naturalized in the United States and subject to the jurisdiction thereof, are citizens of the United States and of the State wherein they reside. No State shall make or enforce any law which shall abridge the privileges or immunities of citizens of the United States; nor shall any State deprive any person of life, liberty, or property, without due process of law; nor deny to any person within its jurisdiction the equal protection of the laws.

Section 2. Representatives shall be apportioned among the several States according to their respective numbers, counting the whole number of persons in each State, excluding Indians not taxed. But when the right to vote at any election for the choice of electors for President and Vice President of the United States, Representatives in Congress, the Executive and Judicial officers of a State, or the members of the Legislature thereof, is denied to any of the male inhabitants of such State, being twenty-one years of age, and citizens of the United States, or in any way abridged, except for participation in rebellion, or other crime, the basis of representation therein shall be reduced in the proportion which the number of such male citizens shall bear to the whole number of male citizens twenty-one years of age in such State.

Section 3. No person shall be a Senator or Representative in Congress, or elector of President and Vice President, or hold any office, civil or military, under the United States, or under any State, who, having previously taken an oath, as a member of Congress, or as an officer of the United States, or as a member of any State legislature, or as an executive or judicial officer of any State, to support the Constitution of the United States, shall have engaged in insurrection or rebellion against the same, or given aid or comfort to the enemies thereof. But Congress may by a vote of two-thirds of each House, remove such disability.

Section 4. The validity of the public debt of the United States, authorized by law, including debts incurred for payment of pensions and bounties for services in suppressing insurrection or rebellion, shall not be questioned. But neither the United States nor any State shall assume or pay any debt or obligation incurred in aid of insurrection or rebellion against the United States, or any claim for the loss or emancipation of any slave; but all such debts, obligations and claims shall be held illegal and void.

Section 5. The Congress shall have power to enforce, by appropriate legislation, the provisions of this article.

THE FIFTEENTH AMENDMENT
TO THE CONSTITUTION OF THE UNITED STATES, 1870

Adopted in 1870, this constitutional amendment prevents states and the federal government from blocking a person's right to vote. Yet Southern states found ways to get around this amendment in order to keep African Americans away from election polls. The passing of the Voting Rights Act of 1965, nearly one hundred years later, restored the ability of black citizens to vote freely.

Section 1. The right of citizens of the United States to vote shall not be denied or abridged by the United States or by any State on account of race, color, or previous condition of servitude.

Section 2. The Congress shall have power to enforce this article by appropriate legislation.

THE CIVIL RIGHTS ACT OF 1875

This law stated that all people, regardless of race, were entitled to full and equal employment. It also guaranteed every person's right to enter businesses and public places, such as hotels, trains, theaters, and parks. In 1883 the Supreme Court ruled that the act was unconstitutional. More than eighty years later, the Civil Rights Act of 1964 reestablished civil rights for African Americans and all U.S. citizens.

Whereas it is essential to just government we recognize the equality of all men before the law, and hold that it is the duty of government in its dealings with the people to mete out equal and exact justice to all, of whatever nativity, race, color, or persuasion, religious or political; and it being the appropriate object of legislation to enact great fundamental principles into law: Therefore,

Be it enacted, That all persons within the jurisdiction of the United States shall be entitled to the full and equal enjoyment of the accommodations, advantages, facilities, and privileges of inns, public conveyances on land or water, theaters, and other places of public amusement; subject only to the conditions and limitations established by law, and applicable alike to citizens of every race and color, regardless of any previous condition of servitude.

Section 2. That any person who shall violate the foregoing section by denying to any citizen, except for reasons by law applicable to citizens of every race and color, and regardless of any previous condition of servitude, the full enjoyment of any of the accommodations, advantages, facilities, or privileges in said section enumerated, or by aiding or inciting such denial, shall, for every such offense, forfeit and pay the sum of five hundred dollars to the person aggrieved thereby, . . . and shall also, for every such offense, be deemed guilty of a misdemeanor, and, upon conviction thereof, shall be fined not less than five hundred nor more than one thousand dollars, or shall be imprisoned not less than thirty days nor more than one year. . . .

Section 3. That the district and circuit courts of the United States shall have exclusively of the courts of the several States, cognizance of all crimes and offenses against, and violations of, the provisions of this act. . . .

Section 4. That no citizen possessing all other qualifications which are or may be prescribed by law shall be disqualified for service as grand or petit juror in any court of the United States, or of any State, on account of race, color, or previous condition of servitude; and any officer or other person charged with any duty in the selection or summoning of jurors who shall exclude or fail to summon any citizen for the cause aforesaid shall, on conviction thereof, be deemed guilty of a misdemeanor, and be fined not more than five thousand dollars.

Section 5. That all cases arising under the provisions of this act . . . shall be renewable by the Supreme Court of the United States, without regard to the sum in controversy.

SOURCE NOTES

p. 5 Leon Litwack, *Been in the Storm So Long: The Aftermath of Slavery* (New York: Vintage Books, 1979), 104.

p. 6 Ibid., 3.

p. 9 James Mellon, ed., *Bullwhip Days: The Slaves Remember, an Oral History* (New York: Avon, 1988), 18–19.

p. 10 Ibid., 18.

p. 12 Eric Foner, *Reconstruction: America's Unfinished Revolution, 1863–1877* (New York: Harper & Row, 1988), 26.

p. 13 Litwack, 5.

p. 15 "The Emancipation Proclamation," n.d., http://www.nara.gov/exhall/featured/ cument/eman/emanproc.html> (May 2003).

p. 15 Saul K. Padover, ed., *On America and the Civil War* (New York: McGraw-Hill, 1971), 222.

p. 16 Litwack, 107.

p. 17 W. E. B. Du Bois, *Black Reconstruction, 1860–1880* (1935; reprint, New York: Meridian Books, 1969), 91.

p. 18 Litwack, 64.

p. 19 Ibid., 65.

p. 19 Ibid., 4.

p. 20 Ibid., 109.

p. 20 Ibid., 109.

p. 21 Ibid., 122.

p. 21 Foner, 70.

p. 22 Litwack, 219.

p. 22 Ibid., 220.

p. 24 Du Bois, *Black Reconstruction, 1860–1880,* 220.

p. 25 Foner, 76.

p. 26 Ibid., 78.

p. 26 Ibid., 77.

p. 27 Ibid., 223.

p. 27 Ibid., 223.

p. 28 Ibid., 223.

p. 28 Ibid., 77.

p. 29 Ibid., 78.

p. 30 A. K. McClure, *Our American Presidents and How We Make Them* (New York: Harper & Brothers, 1902), 201.

p. 30 Litwack, 229.

p. 33 Ibid., 241.

p. 34 Ibid., 242.

p. 36 Ibid., 230.

p. 36 Foner, 103.

p. 37 Ibid., 103.

p. 37 Ibid., 103.

p. 37 Ibid., 103.

p. 37 Ibid., 104.

p. 39 Ibid., 85.

p. 39 Ibid., 86.

p. 39 Ibid., 85.

p. 39 Ibid., 85.

p. 40 Litwack, 531.

p. 40 Ibid., 531.

p. 40 Lerone Bennett Jr., *Before the Mayflower: A History of Black America* (New York: Viking/ Penguin Books, 1984), 217.

p. 45 McClure, 502.

p. 45 John Hope Franklin, and Albert A. Moss Jr., *From Slavery to Freedom: A History of African Americans* (Boston: McGraw-Hill, 2000), 217.

p. 48 Litwack, 402.

p. 48 Bennett Jr., 217.

p. 48 Foner, 105.

p. 49 Ibid., 109.

p. 50 Foner, 105.

p. 50 Ibid., 105.

p. 52 Litwack, 403.

p. 53 Ibid., 403.

p. 53 Ibid., 413

p. 54 Ibid., 393.

p. 54 Ibid., 413.

p. 55 Ibid., 413.

p. 58 Ibid., 502.

p. 58 Ibid., 451.

p. 60 Ibid., 465.

p. 63 Ibid., 473.

p. 64 Ibid., 473.

p. 65 Ibid., 478–479.

p. 66 Ibid., 97.

p. 66 Foner, 99.

p. 67 Ibid., 96.

p. 67 Litwack, 473.

p. 68 Foner, 97.

p. 69 Litwack, 486.

p. 69 Ibid., 486.

p. 69 Ibid., 487.

p. 71 Ibid., 541.

p. 71 Ibid., 542.

p. 71 W. E. B. Du Bois, *The Souls of Black Folk* (1903; reprint, New York: Penguin, 1994), 3–4.

p. 72 John David Smith, *Black Voices from Reconstruction, 1865–1877* (Gainesville: University Press of Florida, 1997), 133.

p. 73 Foner, 79–80.

p. 73 Litwack, 144.

p. 74 George Brown Tindall, *America: A Narrative History,* 2nd ed., Vol. II (New York: W. W. Norton & Company, 1988), 708.

p. 75 Theodore B. Wilson, *The Black Codes of the South* (Tuscaloosa, AL: University of Alabama Press, 1965), 71.

p. 75 Du Bois, *Black Reconstruction in America,* 166.

p. 76 Wilson, 70.

p. 78 Foner, 121.

p. 79 Tindall, 722–723.

p. 80 Mellon, 400.

p. 81 Ibid., 393.

p. 81 Smith, 127.

p. 83 Tindall, 725.

p. 84 Foner, 602.

p. 89 Quoted in Tindall, 751.

p. 90 Mary Wilkin, ed., "Some Papers of the American Cotton Planters' Association, 1865–1866," *Tennessee Historical Quarterly,* March 1949, 49–50.

p. 91 U.S. Congress, Senate, Committee on Education and Labor, *Report of the Committee of the Senate upon the Relations between Labor and Capital, and Testimony Taken by the Committee,* 4 vols., (1885; reprint, New York: Arno Press, 1976), 605.

p. 94 U.S. National Records and Archives Administration, "The Emancipation Proclamation, a Transcription" *Featured Documents,* n.d., <http://www.archives.gov/exhibit_hall/featured_documents/emancipation_proclamation/transcript.html> (September 2003).

p. 97 "Fourteenth Amendment to the U.S. Constitution: Civil Rights (1868)—Transcripts," *OurDocuments.gov,* n.d., <http://www.ourdocuments.gov/content.php?page=transcript&doc=4> (September 3, 2003).

p. 98 "Fifteenth Amendment to the U.S. Constitution: Voting Rights (1870)—Transcripts," *OurDocuments.gov,* n.d., <http://www.ourdocuments.gov/content.php?page=transcript&doc=4> (September 3, 2003).

p. 99 "The Civil Rights Act of 1875," *Civil Rights Act of 1875,* n.d., <http://chnm.gmu.edu/courses/122/recon/civilrightsact.html> (September 2003).

SELECTED BIBLIOGRAPHY

Anderson, Eric, and Alfred A. Moss Jr., eds. *The Facts of Reconstruction: Essays on Honor of John Hope Franklin*. Baton Rouge: Louisiana State University Press, 1991.

Bennett, Lerone Jr. *Before the Mayflower: A History of Black America*. New York: Viking/Penguin Books, 1984.

Berry, Mary Francis, and John W. Blassingame. *Long Memory: The Black Experience in America*. New York: Oxford University Press, 1982.

Billings, Edward C. *The Struggle between the Civilization of Slavery and That of Freedom*. New York: Ayer Company Publishers, 1977.

Blassingame, John W. *Slave Testimony: Two Centuries of Letters, Speeches, Interviews, and Autobiographies*. Baton Rouge: Louisiana State University Press, 1977.

Coulter, E. Merton. *The South during Reconstruction, 1865–1877*. Baton Rouge: Louisiana State University Press, 1992.

Du Bois, W. E. B. *Black Reconstruction, 1860–1880*. 1935. Reprint, New York: Meridian Books, 1969.

———. *The Souls of Black Folk*. 1903. Reprint, New York: Penguin, 1994.

Foner, Eric. *Reconstruction: America's Unfinished Revolution, 1863–1877*. New York: Harper & Row, 1988.

Franklin, John Hope. *Reconstruction after the Civil War*. Chicago: University of Chicago Press, 1962.

Franklin, John Hope, and Alfred A. Moss Jr. *From Slavery to Freedom: A History of African Americans*. Boston: McGraw-Hill, 2000.

Golay, Michael. *Reconstruction and Reaction: The Black Experience of Emancipation, 1861–1913*. New York: Facts on File, 1996.

Gutman, Herbert. *The Black Family in Slavery and Freedom, 1750–1925*. New York: Pantheon Books, 1976.

Harding, Vincent. *There Is a River: The Black Struggle for Freedom in America.* New York: Harcourt Press, 1981.

Jenkins, Wilbert J. *Climbing Up to Glory: A Short History of African Americans during the Civil War and Reconstruction.* Wilmington, DE: Scholarly Resources, 2002.

Jones, Jacqueline. *Labor of Love, Labor of Sorrow: Black Women, Work, and the Family from Slavery to the Present.* New York: Vintage Books, 1985.

Levine, Lawrence W. *Black Culture and Black Consciousness: Afro-American Folk Thought from Slavery to Freedom.* New York: Oxford University Press, 1977.

Litwack, Leon. *Been in the Storm So Long: The Aftermath of Slavery.* New York: Vintage Books, 1979.

Mandle, Jay R. *Not Slave, Not Free: The African-American Experience since the Civil War.* Durham, NC: Duke University Press, 1992.

McClure, A. K. *Our American Presidents and How We Make Them.* New York: Harper & Brothers, 1902.

Meier, August, and Elliot Rudwick. *From Plantation to Ghetto.* New York: Farrar, Hill & Wang, 1976.

Mellon, James, ed. *Bullwhip Days: The Slaves Remember, an Oral History.* New York: Avon, 1988.

Myers, Robert Manson. *Children of Pride: A True Story of Georgia and the Civil War.* New Haven, CT: Yale University Press, 1972.

Padover, Saul K., ed. *On America and the Civil War.* New York: McGraw-Hill, 1971.

Roark, James. *Masters without Slaves.* New York: W. W. Norton, 1977.

Smith, John David. *Black Voices from Reconstruction, 1865–1877.* Gainesville, FL: University Press of Florida, 1997.

Stampp, Kenneth. *Era of Reconstruction, 1865–1877.* New York: Vintage Books, 1967.

Sterling, Dorothy, ed. *The Trouble They Seen: The Story of Reconstruction in the Words of African Americans.* New York: Da Capo Books, 1994.

Tindall, George Brown. *America: A Narrative History.* 2nd ed. Vol. II. New York: W. W. Norton & Company, 1988.

U.S. Congress. Senate. Committee on Education and Labor. *Report of the Committee of the Senate upon the Relations between Labor and Capital, and Testimony Taken by the Committee.* 4 vols. 1885. Reprint, New York: Arno Press, 1976.

U.S. National Archives and Records Administration, "The Emancipation Proclamation," *Featured Documents,* n.d., <http://www.archives.gov/exhibit_hall/featured_documents/emancipation_proclamation/index.html> (September 2003).

Wayne, Michael. *The Reshaping of Plantation Society.* Baton Rouge: Louisiana State University Press, 1983.

Wilkin, Mary, ed. "Some Papers of the American Cotton Planters' Association, 1865–1866." *Tennessee Historical Quarterly,* March 1949.

Williamson, Joel. *The Crucible of Race: Black-White Relations in the American South since Emancipation.* New York: Oxford University Press, 1984.

Wilson, Theodore B. *The Black Codes of the South.* Tuscaloosa, AL: University of Alabama Press, 1965.

FURTHER READING AND WEBSITES

BOOKS

Arnold, James R., and Roberta Arnold. *Divided in Two: The Road to Civil War, 1861.* Minneapolis: Lerner Publications Company, 2002. This title explores the social and political differences that led to the American Civil War.

————. *Life Goes On: The Civil War at Home, 1861–1865.* Minneapolis: Lerner Publications Company, 2002. This book examines the day-to-day experiences of families in the North and South during the war.

————. *Lost Cause: The End of the Civil War, 1864–1865.* Minneapolis: Lerner Publications Company, 2002. This volume focuses on the final year of the war, surrender, and the beginning of Reconstruction.

————. *On to Richmond: The Civil War in the East, 1861–1862.* Minneapolis: Lerner Publications Company, 2002. This book discusses the Civil War experience in the Western United States.

————. *River to Victory: The Civil War in the West, 1861–1863.* Minneapolis: Lerner Publications Company, 2002. This title describes the Civil War experience in the Eastern United States.

————. *This Unhappy Country: The Turn of the Civil War, 1863.* Minneapolis: Lerner Publications Company, 2002. This volume focuses on the decisive battles of the Civil War.

Banfield, Susan. *The Fifteenth Amendment: African-American Men's Right to Vote.* Berkeley Heights, NJ: Enslow, 1998. This book looks at the people behind the passage of the Fifteenth Amendment to the U.S. Constitution and the changes brought about by its passage.

Becker, Helaine. *Frederick Douglass.* Woodbridge, CT: Blackbirch Press, 2001. This book is a biography of one of the foremost leaders in the fight to abolish slavery before the Civil War and to establish the rights of African Americans after emancipation.

Damon, Duane. *Growing Up in the Civil War.* Minneapolis: Lerner Publications Company, 2003. This book presents daily life during the Civil War from the perspective of American children.

Greene, Meg. *Slave Young, Slave Long: The American Slave Experience.* Minneapolis: Lerner Publications Company, 1999. This title presents a social and cultural history of the American slave experience.

Havelin, Kate. *Ulysses S. Grant.* Minneapolis: Lerner Publications Company, 2004. This book is a biography of the Union general and eighteenth president of the United States, whose term lasted through the end of Reconstruction.

Henry, Christopher E. *Forever Free: From the Emancipation Proclamation to the Civil Rights Bill of 1875.* Philadelphia: Chelsea House, 1995. This history describes life for African American soldiers during the Civil War, including the discrimination they faced from some people in the North, as well as the struggles faced by African Americans after the war ended.

Holford, David M. *Lincoln and the Emancipation Proclamation in American History.* Berkely Heights, NJ: Enslow, 2002. Holford focuses on Abraham Lincoln's years as president, highlighting his historic passage of the Emancipation Proclamation.

Hudson, David L. *The Fourteenth Amendment: Equal Protection under the Law.* Berkeley Heights, NJ: Enslow, 2002. This book is a history of the Fourteenth amendment, including its uses in modern times.

Hughes, Christopher. *Andrew Johnson.* Woodbridge, CT: Blackbirch Press, 2001. This title is a biography of the seventeenth president of the United States who entered office upon the assassination of Abraham Lincoln.

King, Wilma. *Children of the Emancipation.* Minneapolis: Carolrhoda Books, Inc., 2000. This book is a photographic history focusing on the lives of children after the Civil War.

McDaniel, Melissa. *W. E .B. Dubois: Scholar and Civil Rights Activist.* New York: Franklin Watts, 1999. This title is a biography of the African American scholar and activist who was born during the time of Reconstruction and went on to be one of the founding members of the National Association for the Advancement of Colored People (NAACP), the largest and oldest civil rights organization in America.

McKissack, Patricia, and Fredrick McKissack. *Days of Jubilee: The End of Slavery in the United States.* New York: Scholastic, 2003. The author explores the many stages of emancipation for African Americans in the United States, beginning with slaves who were given their freedom to fight during the Revolutionary War to African Americans freed by the Thirteenth Amendment to the U.S. Constitution.

McPherson, James. *Fields of Fury: The American Civil War.* New York: Atheneum, 2002. Pulitzer Prize-winning Civil War historian James McPherson provides an introduction to the Civil War.

Naden, Corinne, and Rose Blue. *Civil War Ends: Assassination, Reconstruction, and the Aftermath: The House Divided.* Austin, TX: Raintree/Steck-Vaughan, 1999. This book discusses of the effects that Lincoln's death had on the nation and the challenge the country faced as it struggled to reunite.

Roberts, Jeremy. *Abraham Lincoln.* Minneapolis: Lerner Publications Company, 2004. This title is a biography of President Abraham Lincoln, the sixteenth president of the United States, whose terms included the Civil War and whose policies set in motion the earliest period of Reconstruction.

WEBSITES

Blanche K. Bruce. <http://www.csusm.edu/Black_Excellence/documents/pg-b-bruce.html>. This site is dedicated to the biography of the first black person to serve a full term in the U.S. Senate.

The Emancipation Proclamation. <http://www.archives.gov/exhibit_hall/featured_documents/emancipation_proclamation/index.html>. See and read the famous document written by President Abraham Lincoln.

The Freedman's Bureau Online. <http://freedmensbureau.com/>. Visit this site for a brief description of the Freedman's Bureau, with links to records kept by the Bureau throughout the South.

Hiram Revels. <http://statelibrary.dcr.state.nc.us/nc/bio/afro/revels.htm>. This site presents the biography of the first African American member of Congress.

The Impeachment of Andrew Johnson. <http://www.impeach-andrew johnson.com/>. Learn more about the battle over Reconstruction during Johnson's presidency. A "Who Was Who" link includes brief biographies and portraits of key players, such as Charles Sumner, Benjamin Wade, and Thaddeus Stevens.

P. B. S. Pinchback. <http://www.sec.state.la.us/46.htm>. Listen to a spoken biography of Louisiana's first African American governor.

Primary Documents on the Reconstruction Period. <http://www.multied.com/documents/reconstruction.html>. Study the Reconstruction through documents such as the 1865 law that created the Freedman's Bureau and the Civil Rights Act of 1866.

World Book Encyclopedia. <http://www2.worldbook.com/features/features.asp?feature=aajourney&page=html/bh054.html&direct=yes>. "The African American Journey: Reconstruction" page includes a description of Reconstruction as well as links to useful websites on the Black Codes and the Fourteenth and Fifteenth Amendments.

INDEX

ACKNOWLEDGMENTS

The photographs and illustrations in this book are used with the permission of: © Hulton|Archive by Getty Images, pp. 2–3, 42; Library of Congress, pp. 6, 10, 11, 13, 14, 16, 17, 21, 22, 25 (left and right), 26, 28, 29, 31, 40, 41, 43, 46 (left and right), 47, 48, 50, 57 (right), 58, 59, 60, 62, 64, 73, 74, 75, 76, 79, 81, 82, 85 (left and right), 87, 95; Independent Picture Service, p. 7; © Collection of the New-York Historical Society, p. 8; National Archives, pp. 9, 57 (left); Rare Book and Special Collections Division, Library of Congress, p. 12; © CORBIS, pp. 20, 45, 52, 72, 84, 89; Laura Westlund, p. 23; © Leib Image Archives, pp. 27, 67, 68; Schomburg Center for Research in Black Culture, Photographs and Prints Division, pp. 32, 44, 78, 88; Robert N. Dennis Collection of Stereoscopic Views. Miriam and Ira D. Wallach Division of Art, Prints & Photographs. The New York Public Library, Astor, Lennox and Tilden Foundations, pp. 33, 55; Penn School Collection. Permission granted by Penn Center, Inc. St Helena Island, South Carolina, pp. 35 (left), 37; Ohio Historical Center Archives Library, pp. 35 (right), 70, 77; State Department of Archives and History, Raleigh, North Carolina, p. 38; Federal Writers' Project, USPA, Manuscript Division, Library of Congress, p. 51; Massachusetts Commandery Military Order of the Loyal Legion and the U.S. Army Military History Institute, p. 61; Moorland Spingarn Research Center, Howard University, p. 65; © Bettmann/ CORBIS, pp. 80, 86; Sheet Music Collection, The John Hay Library, Brown University Library, Rhode Island, p. 91.

Cover: © Schomburg Center, the New York Public Library/Art Resource, NY.

TITLES FROM THE AWARD-WINNING PEOPLE'S HISTORY SERIES:

For more information, please call 1-800-328-4929 or visit www.lernerbooks.com